BUSINESS TO BUSINESS GUIDES

GERMAN

BUSINESS TO BUSINESS GUIDES

GERMAN

BY
CHARLES BERLITZ

A Perigee Book

Perigee Books
are published by
The Berkley Publishing Group
200 Madison Avenue
New York, New York 10016

Library of Congress Cataloging-in-Publication Data

Berlitz, Charles, date.
  Business to business in German / by Charles Berlitz — 1st Perigee ed.
  p. cm.
  ISBN: 0-399-51832-0

1. German language — Business German. 2. German language — Textbooks for
foreign speakers — English. 3. German language — Conversation and phrase
books (for merchants) 4. Germany — Commerce. I. Title.
PF3120.C7B47   1994   93-27341 CIP
483.2'421'02465—dc20

Cover design by Bob Silverman, Inc.

Printed in the United States of America
1 2 3 4 5 6 7 8 9 10

CONTENTS

HISTORY

1

German history is full of contradictions. For years, "Germany" itself did not exist; the territory we now call German was home first to a disparate group of tribes, then to a warring band of petty states. The nation of Germany was unified relatively late in European terms – then went on to become a major world military power in two world wars – and then became disunited once again. For years, Germans were justifiably proud of their country and their heritage, reminding themselves and the world that theirs was the country of Beethoven and Goethe. Then, after World War II, many Germans saw their historical tradition in quite a different light, preferring to think of themselves as making a fresh start, whether through "socialist reconstruction" or through the capitalist-sponsored prosperity of the West.

Today, German history is still a source of contention. But with reunification, Germans on both sides of the old Berlin Wall are beginning once again to reconsider their heritage and examine their past. Foreign business travelers would do well to have a sense of German traditions for the light they may shed on Germany today.

PRE-MODERN GERMANY
THE HANSEATIC LEAGUE

In 1241, previously isolated German tribes undertook an historic step: under the leadership of the town of Lübeck, several North German towns united into a trading federation that by 1358 finally became known as the Hanseatic League.

The League was named after the Hanse – German companies of merchants engaged in foreign trade. It was in a sense the world's first trading monopoly: together, the cities in the League set prices and trading practices and agreed not to compete with one another. The arrangements they made gave them a clear competitive advantage over cities outside the League, so that eventually more than 70 cities became members.

The League flourished for many years. In 1370, it won a monopoly over Scandinavian trade. Hanseatic traders pushed overland into Europe as well, linking up with Italian traders and connecting Central Europe with the Mediterranean. It was the sea trade, however, that caused the Hanseatic League to flourish, with the North or Baltic Sea cities of Lübeck, Hamburg, and Bremen becoming the strongest powers in the League. Frankfurt, with its key position on the Main river, was another key League city.

Despite the Hansas' strength, though, they never completely controlled trade on the Baltic Sea. And in about 1430, the Danes realized that there was money to be made from their control of the sea routes around Jutland, and began to charge heavy tolls on ships that sailed into the Baltic. At first this decision helped the land-trading cities in the Hanseatic League, giving them an advantage over countries that traded only by sea. Eventually, however, the League was weakened by the reopening of the Western Seaways of the Mediterranean and the growing power of the Italian city-state. The League was also hurt by the change in the migration pattern of the North Sea herring, which in the early 15th century stopped migrating to Lübeck and the Baltic and remained instead in the North Sea. At that time, the Dutch reaped the benefit of the North Sea herring, at the Hansas' expense.

The final nail in the Hansas' coffin was the 14th century's Black Plague, a catastrophe that destroyed almost one-quarter of the population of Europe. In the wake of this terrifying devastation, travel and trade were disrupted throughout Europe, and the Hansas' power declined.

Modern historians see the Hanseatic League as a kind of precursor of modern capitalist attitudes toward trade. Perhaps it is characteristic of Germany that, at one and the same time, its territory housed both the advanced trading organization of the Hanseatic League and the feudal divisions of barely Christianized tribes throughout the rest of Germany. The existence of advanced capitalist and primitive feudal economies side by side typifies the historical contradictions of Germany's political and economic life.

EARLY MODERN GERMANY

Germany hosted another set of contradictions in the 16th century, as it became both the land of the Protestant Reformation and a country of peasant revolts. Throughout the latter half of the 15th century, the entire Catholic world had witnessed a growing dissatisfaction with the power of the Church. The rise of commerce and the growth of the middle class led to frustration with heavily centralized and traditional power that the Church represented, while the growing power of the German feudal princes brought them into conflict with the political dominance of the Holy Roman Emperor.

Then, on October 31, 1517, Martin Luther posted 95 theses on the church door at Wittenberg, decrying corruption within the Catholic Church and calling for reform. Luther's attack on both the Church's authority and its doctrines led to his open break with it in 1520, as the founder of Protestantism preached the doctrine of salvation by faith alone, rather than through the Catholic route of sacraments, good works, and meditation. Luther's doctrine called for direct communication between humans and God, rather than the mediated communication via Catholic hierarchy and by means of sacramental offices. The more individualist emphasis of Luther's creed appealed both to the rising middle classes and to the warring German princes, and his teachings spread quickly throughout Germany and Scandinavia.

Continued political conflicts between the Lutherans and the Catholic Emperor Charles V made for bitter battles on German territory. Peasant revolts in the 1520s spoke to the people's dissatisfaction with the Church; after the temporary Peace of Augsburg in 1555, the Thirty Years War ravaged the German countryside from 1618 to 1648, as Catholics and Protestants struggled for political control throughout Europe. Although this devastating conflict involved most of Europe, it was fought primarily on German soil, and by the time of the Peace of Westphalia in 1648, German agriculture, commerce, and industry were all in ruins. The Holy Roman Empire had become a mere political shell, and France began to emerge as the dominant European power.

CHANCELLORS AND KINGS

Germany's challenge to France's dominance came in the middle of the 18th century, under the reign of King Frederick the Great (1740-1786). Frederick was the ruler of Prussia, the North German province that for centuries was the most powerful region of Germany and the birthplace for many of Germany's most powerful rulers. Frederick the Great is known as a enlightened or benevolent despot whose promotion of legal and social reforms helped bring Germany into the modern era. He believed strongly in religious liberty and was a good friend of the materialist French philosopher Voltaire. Under Frederick, Prussia consolidated its ascendancy over the rest of Germany. Frederick also set an influential political pattern for Germany, in which a powerful leader makes a "revolution from above," implementing reforms and modernization that may not be fully supported by the economic and political development of the people below.

Frederick died just a few years before the French Revolution of 1789, a political event whose ramifications were felt throughout Europe. The French Republic soon found itself at war with feudal Germany, a war that continued in various forms until the defeat of the French emperor Napoleon in 1815. In that year, Germany was not a unified nation, but a disparate group of petty states, each with its own monarchy and aristocracy. In the face of the growing national power of both France and England, the German states joined with Austria to form the German Confederation, a political grouping that was dominated by Prussia and Austria.

Germany's next "revolution from above" came under Otto von Bismarck. Prussia's Kaiser Wilhelm I made Bismarck his premier in 1862, whereupon Bismarck promptly dissolved parliament and levied taxes for the Prussian Army, moves that were both illegal and unconstitutional. Bismarck's goal was to unify Germany under Prussian rule. To do so, he was ready to split the German Confederation and expel Austria in order that Prussia be the only dominant power in Germany. To this end, he provoked war with Denmark in 1864 and two years later with Austria. When Austria lost the Austro-Prussian War, Bismarck's power was consolidated in Northern Germany via the North German Federation, from which Austria was excluded.

Bismarck went on to exploit Germany's fear of France, provoking the Franco-Prussian War of 1870–1871. On France's humiliating defeat, Bismarck's path to the unification of Germany was clear. He was able to bring all German states into the Prussian orbit, under the rule of William I (Kaiser Wilhelm), with himself as chancellor. Thus Bismarck had finally united Germany into a modern political state – with himself as virtual dictator.

Bismarck's career speaks again to the ironies of German history. Because of the growth of the socialist movement in Germany's expanding industrial sector, Bismarck was moved to implement a great many social reforms, including maximum-hours legislation, child-labor laws, and extensive benefits in case of sickness, old age, and unemployment. In fact, although Germany was still a monarchy, its economic policies were the envy of the French and

British democracies, for in many ways Bismarck's fear of labor unrest had led him to grant workers more rights than they had elsewhere. The combination of advanced social policies with an authoritarian political system would continue to be typical of German society.

Bismarck was finally removed from power in 1890, two years after his enemy Kaiser Wilhelm II succeeded to the throne. His legacy remained, however, not least in the German colonies he had acquired in Africa and the Middle East, as well as in the complicated system of ententes and alliances that he had helped to construct throughout Europe.

GERMANY AT WAR

The alliances of Bismarck and his successors were one major cause of World War I, whose outbreak in 1914 found Germany allied with Austria against the powerful combination of Britain, France, and Russia. When the United States eventually joined the Allies, it was able to defeat Germany in 1918, ushering in the heavy reparations and debts of the Treaty of Versailles.

The economic desolation resulting from World War I and the subsequent reparations left Germany in turmoil throughout the 1920s. On the one hand, pro-democracy forces constructed the Weimar Republic; on the other hand, Adolf Hitler's National Socialism exploited unemployment and depression to mobilize the powerful anti-democratic forces of fascism. Eventually, Hitler rose to become chancellor of Germany in 1933, a position that he used to become the most powerful dictator Germany had ever known. His suspension of civil rights combined with apparent economic reform seemed to many at the time to be a kind of echo of Bismarck, although in fact Hitler's brutal suppression of political freedom and his utilization of German finance and industry went far beyond anything Bismarck had ever imagined.

In the years 1938 and 1939, Hitler began to expand German territories. When he annexed Austria, observers were able to rationalize this action in light of Germany's previous moves toward expanding and consolidating its national base. When France and Britain met Hitler at Munich to discuss his taking of the Sudetenland, they likewise rationalized their agreement by references to Germany's history. In 1939, however, German troops occupied the remainder of Czechoslovakia, where German-speaking inhabitants were few in number. When Germany invaded Poland in September 1939, Britain and France declared war, only to suffer the defeat of France in 1940.

World War II pitted Germany, Italy and Japan against Britain and her allies, which eventually included the Soviet Union and the U.S.A. Much of Germany's war effort was directed against the Soviet Union; the vast majority of Allied casualties were men lost on the Eastern Front. When the tide of war finally began to turn in 1943, it was the Soviet Union whose troops marched westward to liberate Poland, Czechoslovakia, and the rest of Eastern Europe. But the Soviet Union and the other major allied powers had their own conflicts; Germany had been defeated by two warring world camps.

GERMANY'S DIVISION

When Germany was defeated at the end of World War II, it was occupied by all four major Allies: the United States, France, Great Britain, and the Soviet Union. The first three powers were united in their devotion to capitalist economic structures, whereas the Soviet Union wanted to promote socialism, both in Germany and in the Eastern European nations that it had liberated and was now continuing to occupy. The strongest Communist movement in Central and Eastern Europe before the war had been in Germany. Thus there was some basis for the Soviets' effort to create a Communist nation out of the German zone that they occupied after the war.

Because the Soviets had entered Germany from the east, they occupied the segment of Germany that contained Berlin, the former capital of Germany and Prussia. However, Berlin, too, had been occupied by all four powers, so that only one portion of it was Soviet-occupied. In 1948 and 1949, the Soviets blockaded Berlin, hoping to affirm the principle that the entire city remain within their zone of occupation. The Allies retaliated by airlifting food and supplies to so-called West Berlin, which was finally established as a separate entity, politically bound to West Germany (the Federal Republic of Germany), despite its being completely surrounded by the territory of Communist East Germany (the Democratic Republic of Germany, or GDR).

So Germany resumed its career as a divided country in 1949, the year that the Federal Republic of Germany (FRG) was officially created. When the North Atlantic Treaty Organization (NATO) was formed in 1955 to strengthen European efforts against the Soviet Union, the FRG joined promptly, placing itself firmly in the United States camp of the Cold War. That was also the year that the FRG gained its full sovereignty, although of course the United States continued to exert a major influence in both foreign and domestic policy.

In 1957, the nations of Western Europe formed the European Economic Community (Common Market). The FRG joined as founder member, signaling both its loyalty to the United States and its determination to regain Germany's former economic power.

The FRG's first chancellor was Konrad Adenauer, whose anti-Communist, pro-U.S., and Cold War policies continued to dominate West German politics until his retirement in 1963. Adenauer also presided over West Germany's rapid recovery of prosperity, an economic growth based on American Marshall Aid, on modernization, and on an efficient use of the latest technological advances, and fueled by the postwar bans on German military expansion, which left resources free for domestic purposes.

The 1960s were stormy times for Germany politically. Since 1952, a fortified fence had prevented East Germans from crossing the border to the FRG. But Berlin was still undivided. In 1961, the East Germans, angered by the rapid emigration of their people through Berlin to the West, built the infamous Berlin Wall, an actual barrier dividing the city into its political halves. Conflicts between the two Germanys, as well as between the United States and the Soviet Union, continued to ruffle the otherwise smooth surface of Germany's postwar recovery.

Adenauer had been a Christian Democrat, a conservative, in German politics. When Willy Brandt became chancellor in 1969, he began the period of Social Democratic–Liberal (or Free Democratic) coalition rule of the FRG. Brandt ushered in a period of eased relations with both East Germany and the Soviet Union, as well as presiding over domestic reforms that improved wages and benefits for industrial workers and liberalized other social policies. The Social Democrats' decisive victory in 1972 was seen as their mandate to embark on a number of reforms.

The Social Democrats were able to retain power even in 1974, when a senior official in Brandt's office was found to be an East German spy. Brandt was forced to resign over the Günther Guillaume affair, but his former defense minister, Helmut Schmidt, continued the reign of the Social Democratic–Liberal coalition when he assumed the office of chancellor.

Throughout the 1970s, the FRG was seen as a kind of postwar economic miracle. In contrast to the economic difficulties of the GDR, the FRG's prosperity was seen as justifying capitalist economic policy. In addition, NATO's and the United States' assumption of military responsibility for Germany provided a much-needed boost for the FRG's economy.

However, in 1979, Germany too fell prey to the worldwide recession. Continued economic problems undermined the leadership of the Social Democrats to such an extent that in 1982 the Free Democrats switched sides and the conservative Christian Democrat Helmut Kohl came to power as chancellor.

The general election of 1983 confirmed Kohl's leadership of West Germany as well as the ascendancy of the Christian Democratic Union (CDU). Interestingly, the same election saw the emergence of the so-called "Greens," a disparate group of environmentalists, socialists, and other inheritors of New Left ideas. Although the Greens seemed unlikely to gain the parliamentary weight of either the Christian Democrats or the Social Democrats, the 1980s would see them play an influential role in German politics as they raised issues, organized demonstrations, and generally acted as a voice of conscience for unpopular issues.

The 1980s worldwide were a time of conservative ascendancy, with President Ronald Reagan in power in the United States and Prime Minister Margaret Thatcher carrying the Conservative banner in Britain. Like Thatcher's Conservatives, Germany's Christian Democrats strongly supported the Reagan presidency as well as U.S. military dominance in the West. The Soviet Union was seen as Europe's major political enemy, and the United States was therefore cast as both Europe's protector and its leader.

Of course, in both Germany and in Britain, many people chafed under the idea that political leadership was coming from outside the country, particularly in questions of nuclear power and troop deployment.

However, like the United States, Germany enjoyed a kind of

economic boom in the 1980s after a conservative government took office, so political criticisms were muted at best.

REUNIFICATION

The next chapter in Germany's history is still being written. Perhaps it might be seen as beginning in 1987, when GDR leader Erich Honecker made his first visit to the FRG, signaling the coming erosion of East–West barriers. As internal reforms within the Soviet Union spread throughout that nation's sphere of influence, the political climate in the Communist states of Eastern Europe was also affected. Eventually, one socialist country after another overthrew its socialist regime to embrace the principles of free-market capitalism and Western political democracy.

In 1989, this process reached East Germany. Thousands emigrated to the West through the newly opened border between Hungary and Austria, forcing the GDR government to agree to the freedom of all its citizens to leave the country if they wished. Taking advantage of this concession, crowds broke down the Berlin Wall on the night of November 9. The way to reunification was open. Although mass demonstrations, especially in Leipzig, brought about Honecker's fall and the advent of reformist Communist governments under Egon Krenz and Hans Modrow, elections held in March 1990 revealed an overwhelming majority of the population in favor of joining the FRG. On October 3, 1990, the two countries were formally reunited, amidst widespread optimism and rejoicing among East Germans.

This heady optimism has not survived the actual process of reunification, however, or at least not to the same extent. Since the FRG had attained so much higher a standard of living than the GDR, at least as far as consumer goods and outward signs of prosperity were concerned, many residents of the GDR believed that reunification would automatically bring them up to the living standards of their West German neighbors. In fact, citizens of the former GDR are finding that reunification has not brought the economic advances that they had expected. Pensions, health benefits, and other "safety net" guarantees turned out to have been far more extensive in the GDR than in the free-market FRG, and the process of standardizing currency has appeared to greatly endanger the social insurance provisions of the GDR. In part this is due to the artificially low prices of the GDR, which had been protected against inflation by means of government subsidies for such staples as basic foodstuffs, rent, and medical care. When these socialist subsidies were removed and new currency standards imposed, GDR citizens found themselves with the worst of both worlds: low socialist wages and high capitalist prices.

The FRG is also nervous about the influx of skilled GDR workers into a market already plagued by an unusually high rate of unemployment for the German economy (although the level is low by U.S. standards). FRG trade unions are particularly anxious, since they know that GDR workers are accustomed to lower wages and are eager for any increase in their ability to purchase consumer goods.

Western business attitudes toward investing in the former East Germany have ranged from cautious to skeptical.

Much to the West's surprise, East Germany's industry and infrastructure turned out to be so hopelessly outdated and overmanned that most of it was beyond any hope of modernization and had to be closed down. The labor force was poorly trained and unfamiliar with modern technology. Unemployment quickly reached massive proportions, and labor unrest mounted as East German wages remained substantially below those in the West.

With a worldwide economic recession and a shrinking worldwide market for consumer goods, Western business interest has not yet determined where the new Germany fits into its overall plan.

Certainly reunification of Germany will bring many new economic opportunities both inside and outside the country. What new political and economic developments will emerge from this latest chapter of German history remain to be seen.

GERMAN CULTURAL ATTITUDES

To some extent, the last five decades of German history have constituted a kind of massive national identity crisis. During World War II, most German citizens identified with their country at war as do most citizens worldwide. When they were defeated in 1945, however, Germans had to contend not only with the loss of a prolonged and devastating war, but also with the revelations of the horrendous crimes of the Nazi regime. The Nuremberg Trials were only the most dramatic expression of how profoundly Germany's government had been identified with the systematic and brutal destruction of human life, as well as with a frighteningly racist ideology that had been used to promote the idea of German national superiority.

Germans reacted to these revelations in various ways. In the GDR, there was some effort to keep the past alive by distancing it as the product of corrupt capitalist trends, as opposed to the current enlightened socialist regime. In the FRG, there was an effort to think of the war as the *Stunde Null*, or zero hour, as though history were beginning again, born again after the horror of the Nazi past. To many in Germany, it was almost as though the FRG were undergoing a kind of forced amnesia, willfully forgetting the events that culminated in war and defeat.

In the 1970s in the FRG, groundbreaking writers such as Heinrich Böll and innovative filmmakers such as Rainer Werner Fassbinder attempted to come to terms with this historical amnesia, creating works that explored the possible links between Germany's past and its present. The troubling questions of German identity were raised in both overt and subtle ways, in both artistic and political arenas.

Of course, the question of German identity was troubling and problematic for other reasons as well. Since Germany was divided in two, and since reunification looked to be so impossible (despite the provision in the West German Constitution committing every government to work for that goal), many Germans wondered in what sense they shared a nationality with East Germany. Reunification has so far done little to diminish the cultural differences which forty years of separation under two different social and political systems have created in the populations of East and West .

In addition, German tradition had always been more identified with region and city than with the nation itself. As we have seen, it was only in 1871 that Germany was unified at all, after years of divisions among feuding petty states and rival aristocracies. Many Germans identify themselves as Bavarians or Saxons before they think of themselves as Germans, possibly because Bavaria and Saxony have longer histories than the entity known as Germany.

To this day, Germany is divided into *Länder*, regions that operate somewhat like states in the United States or provinces in Canada; and, as in many other European nations, it is possible to chart

Germany's political and cultural attitudes by region. The northern part of the country – particularly Hamburg and Bremen – consider themselves more progressive and forward-thinking, partly because of their more developed industrial base and their focus on modern technology. This part of the country has a long tradition of Protestantism, which contributed to its industrial development.

Southern Germany, on the other hand – Bavaria in particular – tends to be far more conservative. This trend has been supported by the more or less unbroken hold of the Catholic Church on the area, as well as the more agricultural focus of the region.

Although Berlin is now potentially able to become a capital as well as a cultural center for the entire nation of Germany, this was not possible for many years, adding further support to Germany's tendency to fragment into regions. Foreign visitors will notice that both Hamburg and Munich have developed their own cultural traditions and identities to an unusual extent for cities of their size.

Interestingly, Germans prize their regional accents and other markers of local identity. Speech accent tends to vary much more by region than by class, creating a somewhat misleading sense of a classless society. Although class and social distinctions in Germany are in fact quite rigid, postwar workers in the FRG have come to identify more strongly with bourgeois lifestyles. In addition, the physical devastation caused by the war created a kind *nouveau riche* sector whose wealth was gained since 1945. Although wealth and privilege still exist in Germany (the wage differential between an unskilled worker and a company head is about 4.5), freedom of opportunity has emerged in Germany over the past few decades, disrupting the centuries-old traditions of aristocracy and privilege by birth.

This air of egalitarianism may be misleading, however. Some 50,000 members of Germany's old noble families still use their titles; they continue to socialize with each other and to make the most of their inherited status. Many firms seek out the services of a *Graf* or a *Fürst* to grace their board of directors.

Another factor in German cultural identity is the presence of Turkish "guest workers," immigrants brought into the country in the 1970s and 1980s to do the menial work and lower-paid industrial labor that most native-born Germans are unwilling to do. The presence of large numbers of "foreigners" living and working in Germany created another racial problem, compounded by the massive influx of millions of ethnic Germans from Eastern European countries and asylum-seekers from all over the world in the years immediately following reunification. Many native-born Germans blame these people for their nation's growing economic problems, and racial attacks on them became commonplace in the 1990s.

Once again, the question of reunification poses interesting challenges to Germans as they consider the meaning of German identity. Foreign travelers may find that the 1990s are a time of great flux in Germany, as residents in both East and West come to terms with their new situation. Outsiders would do well both to remember German traditions and to be open to the new traditions that are being invented virtually as they watch.

DOING BUSINESS
WITH THE GERMANS

2

Germany is a highly advanced, technologically developed country, and its consumer styles and product availability often resemble those of other Western countries. This apparent similarity can be deceptive, however; Germany's business attitudes are shaped by a profoundly conservative, traditional approach to work, money, and social relationships. Americans or Britons who operate in Germany as they would at home are likely to find themselves at best misunderstood, at worst shunned.

THE GERMAN WORK ETHIC

Germans have a very strong work ethic: the very word for "lazy" in German – *faul* – also means "foul" or "putrid." The Protestant North in particular values slow, steady, unremitting labor toward the pursuit of a goal, with stolid efficiency being valued far beyond any "flashy" talent for getting rich quick. Older Germans are perhaps understandably even more conservative than their younger counterparts, and apocryphal stories are still told of middle-aged laid-off executives who get up, dress in their business clothes, and leave the house for an entire workday every day, rather than appear to families or neighbors to be unemployed.

Despite the German focus on efficiency, however, the pace of work is not as demanding in Germany as it is elsewhere in the West. Perhaps because of Germany's greater productivity and technology development, Germans in 1988 worked fewer hours per year than any other major industrial power: an average of 1,708 hours per year, as compared to 1,771 in France; 1,778 in the United Kingdom; 1,912 in the United States; and 2,156 in Japan. Postwar prosperity has led to some relaxation in Germany, so that whereas Germans in 1960 worked 56 billion hours, in 1986 they worked only 43 billion hours. However, these hours probably represent more actual work and less socializing than in their industrial counterparts.

This slow but efficient pace emerges in unexpected ways, often misleading foreigners into seeing Germans as either slow-thinking or cold. Neither view is particularly correct. While German receptionists may move more slowly than the New York, London, or Sydney executive is used to, they are invariably efficient and thorough, as are the executives for whom they work. Likewise, German offices operate according to a seemingly endless list of rules and regulations, but far from creating a cold or heartless office atmosphere, the very clarity of expectations allows Germans to relax, sure of what's required of them and of whether they're fulfilling their well-defined duties. Tension and anxiety are rare in workplaces in Germany, despite the practices that may appear formal to foreign eyes.

German companies tend to do things by the book; that is, there is a companywide plan and a long-standing protocol that determines exactly how decisions will be made and how agreements with foreigners will be reached, and this plan and protocol will almost invariably be followed. This can make for lengthly, drawn-out negotiations with foreign firms, particularly because German decisions are generally made by consensus among teams of managers. However, the foreign business partner does have the satisfaction of knowing that once a decision is reached, all of the German corporation's resources will be mobilized to carry it out.

Along with the tendency to operate "by the book" goes a sense of doing business as a kind of moral enterprise, a kind of public service through building a firm and contributing to the economy's slow, steady growth.

Get-rich-quick brilliance and a pioneering spirit are neither valued nor particularly well understood in Germany. Certain financing schemes – junk bonds, floating interest rates, and the like – are viewed with shock and some dismay by many Germans, as are ruthless takeovers and no-holds-barred competition.

In general, Germans look on unsteadiness and innovation with a great deal of mistrust. German politeness may prevent any public display of disapproval, but foreign businesspeople would do well to be aware of the underlying German conservatism and to accommodate to it as far as possible.

GERMAN BUSINESS RELATIONS

In this scheme of things, personal loyalties and closely knit networks of business associates are extremely important, so foreigners should be aware of any efforts to "divide and rule." It is possible – although quite difficult – for foreign business people to penetrate the closed society of German big business, but any attempt to play one company off against another, or one company department against another, will be less likely to provide an opening than to cause all the players to close ranks tightly against foreign "subversion."

Germany has one of the strictest set of antitrust laws in the world. In addition to its own national policy, it must also submit to EC laws prohibiting trusts or cartels. However, within the context of written law is an intricate network of unwritten law, a network in which personal loyalty, rigid hierarchy, deference to authority and tradition, and clearly defined custom all work together to determine business conduct.

For example, in banking, the Deutsche Bank is of course prohibited from holding a monopoly of banking business, and in theory smaller banks are free to strike out on their own any time they like. In practice, however, it is virtually unimaginable that a small German bank would engage in any innovative practice that had not been tacitly ratified by the Deutsche Bank; to know what banks would be likely to accept, Geman executives would invariably look to the top rather than trying out experiments on a smaller scale.

Likewise, companies exact a kind of personal loyalty from employees unheard-of in many parts of the Western world. "Headhunting" is virtually unknown, since executives tend to remain with their companies for years if not for life. Some years ago, foreign banking expanded rapidly and suddenly in Frankfurt, with consequent attempts to woo German bankers away from their old companies. To the surprise of the foreigners, the German managers chose to stay where they were, despite the attractive wage and benefits packages being offered.

In the same vein, Germans tend to be quite attached to their home cities. Many foreign companies choose to locate their overseas branches in Munich, since that is the one German city to which local executives are generally willing to move. The small size of most German cities, combined with the lack of one central business headquarters (even today, Frankfurt is hardly comparable to New York, London, or Paris as a center of the the new German economy), contribute to a pleasantly slow pace of life in German business. Even in Frankfurt or Munich, a businessperson might be at his or her suburban home within half an hour of leaving work, and in a smaller city the pace may feel positively rural. Thus German executives are not likely to relocate either within or outside the country, except in very unusual circumstances.

On the other hand, the lack of a fixed speed limit on most parts of the *Autobahn,* combined with the easy availability of chauffeur-driven Mercedes, gives German executives a different perception of distance. A Bonn–Frankfurt commute is hardly unheard of, and foreign business travelers may also be expected to travel long distances in pursuit of business.

As one might expect, the social circles of German upper management and banking are quite close-knit, and generally difficult for a foreigner to penetrate. Although home and work are rigidly separated, in the sense that business is rarely conducted over a meal or at a social occasion, nonetheless, social events are an important part of the fabric of business life. Thus a foreigner will almost never be invited to a German party, since business won't be discussed there – although the party guests will almost certainly all be part of the upper-management circles of a local community.

Within this tightly bound group of executives, skiing vacations and dinner parties represent important social occasions, as do vacations at Sylt, an island off German's northwest North Sea coast. In fact, many companies maintain a house at Sylt for their executives' use, so that they can freely mingle with the German business elite.

WOMEN IN BUSINESS

German social conservatism affects attitudes toward women, as well. Generally, women are not treated as equals in Germany, and the business and finance worlds tend to reveal an even greater degree of male supremacy than is evident elsewhere in the society. German women have made greater headway in publishing, public relations, and politics than they have in business or banking.

Interestingly, three out of four companies started in Germany are now founded by women, perhaps because starting her own business is almost the only way a German woman can rise in management ranks (the other way is to inherit a position from a husband or father). Possibly the increase in female-run businesses will make some impact on German social attitudes.

Another possible avenue for the change is the women's rights departments in many German cities and *Länder* (states or regions). However, conditions for women are so backward that these departments are primarily concerned with discrimination in pay and in entry-level hiring; it is unclear how long it will be before they get around to dealing with barriers to women's progress in management.

The consequence of this situation for the foreign business-woman is that she is likely to be isolated, both socially and professionally. She should be aware that the politeness she receives will bear no relation to the degree to which she's actually taken seriously. She may need to prepare herself to fight for recognition from German colleagues whose assumptions about women's place are so deep as to go unquestioned.

MEETING WITH GERMANS

German businesspeople believe firmly in face-to-face contact, regardless of whatever new opportunities telecommunications may have opened up. They see business meetings as the key to cementing relationships, and very well may require a personal meeting before going ahead with a business deal.

German business executives will most likely have a clear perception of themselves as the hosts with the foreign businessperson as the guest. In their view, the host should take the lead in developing the relationship and in conducting the meeting. A foreign guest who matched German confidence and aggression in pursuing business would be viewed with some distrust. Although Germans may seem somewhat arrogant to some foreign businesspeople, they will expect their "guests" to show a certain deference.

As we have seen, personal relations and company loyalty are quite important in German business. Elsewhere, a foreign business-person might try to exploit rivalries or divisions within or between companies; pursuing this course in Germany will lead to hostility and a closing of ranks against the foreigner.

Germans place a high value on self-sufficiency – a value that their excellent technical training goes a long way toward supporting. Thus, most German businesses will not rely on outside studies or consultants. Rather, they insist on reviewing a company's technical data for themselves; if further research is necessary, they will almost almost certainly conduct it in-house.

Because Germans believe deeply in politeness, it may be difficult for the foreign negotiator to divine their actual reaction within a meeting. Since Germans tend to be thorough, however, the foreigner might assume that being hustled quickly through a meeting indicates lack of interest, while being kept for hours going over a myriad of details suggests genuine excitement about a potential deal.

23

Because of their firm division between socializing and work life, Germans rarely have business dinners; certainly it's rare that dinner would be treated as a "working meal." Likewise, because of their early hours, Germans rarely go in for "power breakfasts". If there is a working meal in Germany, it will most likely be a business lunch; business dinners would be reserved for a day when time was so tight as to make such unusual scheduling necessary. It's more likely that a dinner invitation in Germany indicates a very high level of contact or a fairly advanced degree of association, one that the foreign businessperson should prize.

The foreigner wishing to play host to German contacts would do well to select an appropriate restaurant in town before issuing a dinner invitation.

TRADE FAIRS

Perhaps the most useful form of business association in Germany is the trade fair, a form of business contact for which Germany is famous. German firms take these fairs quite seriously, because frequently important deals are made at these national and international meetings. Fairs are particularly important in capital-goods and high-tech industries.

The foreigner who wants to attend a German trade fair should write for the catalog ahead of time. Then he or she should write to the appropriate executives to arrange meetings in advance. German trade organizations or government agencies based in your home country may be helpful in determining which type of information a foreign firm should bring to its presentation at the fair.

GERMAN BUSINESS STRUCTURES

Although Germany's "economic miracle" would seem to be the ultimate product of unrestrained free enterprise, the German business tradition is actually quite conservative and highly regulated. In addition to antitrust (anticartel) legislation imposed by the Allies after 1945, and the antitrust laws of the EC, Germany has its own set of national traditions that serve to mitigate the unrestrained competition that became the hallmark of American, British, and Canadian business in the 1980s.

In one sense, German society is still profoundly shaped by the upheaval of the second world war, which created a kind of nouveau riche society wherein a person from any background might take advantage of economic opportunity if only he or she had the capital. In another very real sense, however, German business is still ruled by the old family-owned firms, reflecting a continuity with Germany's aristocracy. More to the point, only 0.13% of German enterprises are public corporations whose shares are sold openly on the stock market. Germany's old families, along with its bankers, are the real power in the German economy.

Private companies are the major form of German business organization. In Germany, a private limited company is known as a *Gesellschaft mit beschränkter Haftung* or GmbH. Partnerships are another popular form of organization. The least popular form is the public corporation, the *Aktiengesellschaft*, or AG, which sells shares on the stock market in order to expand its capital base.

Each of these three forms of organization has its own structure, discussed here, and its own corporate hierarchy, discussed below. It is of the utmost importance that the foreign business traveler familiarize himself or herself with the structure and hierarchy of potential German business partners, since each type of German organization operates quite differently from its counterpart in the United States or the United Kingdom.

The German GmbH may be a large firm – BASF is one – but small and medium-sized companies have been more likely to organize themselves in this way. For the most part, this form's popularity comes from the far less strict legal regulations under which it operates, as opposed to the strict rules governing the AGs.

A GmbH is fairly easy both to start up and to run. In theory, one person can come up with 50,000 DM for registration – only half of which must actually be paid before registration – and this person can then be both the sole shareholder and the sole director. The Articles of Association of a GmbH must specify the company's major activities, but in very general terms only, so that the cost of setting up a GmbH can be as little as 300 DM for a small business and as low as 7,000 DM for a company capitalized at 1 million DM. To set up a comparably-sized company as an AG could cost up to 21,000 DM, so the savings in this regard are obvious.

In the same vein, the operating costs of a GmbH are also lower, since regulations are again far simpler. If a company employs 500 or more people, a GmbH must have a supervisory board; if a company is smaller, it may be run by its director. Formerly, GmbHs did not even have to submit to annual audits in most cases, although now any firm over a certain size must both conduct an annual audit and publish its accounts.

There are a variety of partnership forms in Germany, of which three are the most common:

The *Kommanditgesellschaft* or KG, is a kind of limited commercial partnership, consisting of one or more limited partner in conjunction with one (or more) general partner. The limited partner has limited liability; the general partner assumes the remainder of the risk. Although this form is far more popular in the United States and Great Britain than it is in Germany, its popularity in Germany is growing.

The *Gesellschaft mit beschränkter Haftung Kommanditgesellschaft*, or GmbH & Co KG, is another form of limited partnership in which the general partner's function is fulfilled by a limited liability company. Shareholders of the GmbH itself may be the other limited partners, so that liability is limited for everyone involved. This form of GmbH & Co KG is actually fairly common.

Observers might wonder why a company would organize as a GmbH & Co KG, rather than as a GmbH, which also has limited liability. The advantage is that the GmbH & Co KG is not taxed; rather, its members are taxed separately on their share of the partnership's profits. The GmbH itself, however, is taxed – and at corporate rates. The difference between individual and corporate rates may make the GmbH & Co KG a far more profitable arrangement. In addition, GmbH & Co KGs are exempt from the EC regulation requiring GmbHs of a certain size to be audited and to publish their accounts.

The *Kommanditgesellschaft auf Aktien* or KGaA is the third common form of partnership in Germany. This form of organization is a separate legal entity in which shareholders play the role of limited partners, with their liability limited to the amount of their investment in a company. Although this is a relatively rare form in Germany, it is the type of organization shown by the chemical company Henkel.

Public corporations, or AGs, operate under a welter of complex and extensive regulations, so that only those companies with very large capital requirements bother to operate in this way. A business must have at least 100,000 DM in capital to form an AG, and 25% of this capital must be paid up before registration. As we have seen, some 20,000 DM is required to meet the startup costs of an AG of this size.

Once an AG is set up, it must demonstrate the existence of at least five shareholders. It must also be run by two boards – one to manage the corporation (the *Vorstand*), the other to supervise operations as would a board of directors (the *Aufsichtsrat*). An *Aufsichtsrat* must have a minimum of three members. A company capitalized up to 3 million DM can have a maximum of 10 members on its *Aufsichtsrat*; the figures go up to 16 and 20 for companies capitalized at up to 20 million DM and above 20 million DM, respectively.

GERMAN CORPORATE HIERARCHIES

The foreign business traveler who is dealing with an AG would do well to understand the function of its two separate boards, since otherwise he or she might be tempted to assume that these boards correspond to similar-sounding entities elsewhere. In fact, the German form of organization is to some extent *sui generis*, and can best be undertood on its own terms.

The *Aufsichtsrat*, the supervisory board, is entirely made up of people who come from outside the corporation. Frequently, representatives of the big banks sit on a company's *Aufsichtsrat*, whether or not their institutions own shares in the company. Lawyers and the representatives of other corporations may also sit on this board. This type of *Aufsichtsrat* member is elected by the company's shareholders, who are responsible for half the board.

The other half of the board is elected by the company's workers, as an example of what the Germans call *Mitbestimmung* – worker participation. In the case of a tie, the board chair – elected by the shareholders – has the deciding vote.

Foreign observers should remember the degree of separation between the *Aufsichtsrat* and the *Vorstand*, which is involved in the day-to-day running of an operation. The *Aufsichtsrat* is removed from daily operations, although it can appoint or remove managers in the *Vorstand*. It must also approve any investments or major strategic moves made by *Vorstand* managers. Its role is to protect shareholders' and workers' interests, which day-to-day managers cannot be counted upon to do.

Of course, the *Vorstand* managers are in the company every day, whereas the *Aufsichtsrat* directors are not. Therefore, in practice, the *Vorstand* managers may indeed have the last word – but always with the awareness of the restraining influence of the *Aufsichtsrat*.

The *Vorstand* is run by a group of six, each of whom is known as a *Vorstandsmitglied*, or management board member. There may also be a chair – *Vorsitzender* – or a spokesperson – *Sprecher* – who operates as a kind of first among equals, rather than a genuine head of the company. Sometimes the term *Vorstandsmitglied* is translated as "Director" or "Senior Vice-President", but, as is evident, these British/American titles do not exactly correspond to the German position.

Each *Vorstandsmitglied* is responsible for a division or function of the company (sometimes, though rarely, two). However, although individuals may supervise particular areas, each area of the company is the responsibility of the board as a whole, so ultimately all decisions are collective ones.

The collective nature of German decision-making – in which neither the *Vorstandsmitglied* assigned to a division, nor the "Chair" or "Spokesperson" has final authority – is crucial for foreign business travelers to understand. Either a consensus or a huge majority of a board must go along with every major decision – including decisions to collaborate with foreign partners – so the would-be foreign partner must appeal to the *Vorstand* as a whole, not simply to its head or to the head of the relevant division. Months may be needed for the *Vorstand* to come to a decision. It is not uncommon for a half or even a whole day per week to be given to the meeting of the *Vorstand* – the *Vorstandssitzung*.

The *Generalbevollmächter* (which translates rather misleadingly as "chief executive") is junior to a member of the *Vorstand*. In fact, the *Generalbevollmächtige* are those in line for appointment to the *Vorstand*, or those serving in another type of key function, such as the firm's lawyer.

At the next level in the hierarchy are *Hauptabteilungsleiter*, each of whom leads major divisions or product lines. Below them are the *Direktoren*, which might seem to translate as "directors," but in fact *Direktoren* are the top level of middle management.

In some firms, the next level down is composed of

Abteilungsleiter, department heads in charge of three or four groups. Each group is headed by a *Gruppenleiter*, who supervises the level of management known as *Prokuristen*. A *Prokurist's* designation suggests that he or she can "sign for the company," although in some cases this not literally true.

As we have seen, private companies do not have this twin-board situation. They have no *Aufsichtsrat*, although they may have a *Beirat*, or advisory board. Their real operational supervisors are the *Geschäftsführung*, a group of general managers chaired by the *Vorsitzender der Geschäftsführung*. An individual on this board is known as a *Geschäftsführer*.

Partnerships in Germany have yet another structure. KgaAs are headed by a managing partner known as the *Geschäftsinhaber*. Small KGs are headed by a *Kommanditist*. The largest German partnerships are headed by a *Hauptabteilungsleiter* or *General-bevollmächtigter*.

FOREIGN INVESTMENT

Germany's interest in attracting foreign investment is reflected in the fact that the country imposes virtually no restrictions on foreign businesses operating or investing within its borders. It is one of the only countries in the world that has no permanent authority charged with overseeing foreign business ventures.

In like vein, investors may own any percentage of equity in a German company, may buy any type of real estate within Germany, and may operate any foreign-owned company there. Both German and foreign firms need licenses for certain types of businesses – insurance, savings banks, and passenger transport.

However, foreign firms face no restrictions on any of the following types of transactions: normal commercial transactions; the transfer of dividends and profits; the transfer of interest on foreign private loans; the remittance of royalties and fees; the repatriation of capital; or the repayment of principal on foreign private loans.

In fact, foreign firms operating in Germany generally prefer to operate through local subsidiaries, since establishing their own branches opens them to complicated accounting requirements as well as to heavier tax burdens. Foreign firms that do want to establish branches must get permission from the *Landesregierung* – the local provincial government – which is generally easy to do.

Otherwise, setup procedures are the same as those followed by German companies.

Any German subsidiary serving a foreign firm must register in the local court's Commercial Register; foreign firms should be aware that if a firm is not registered, any agreements entered into become the sole liability of the parent company.

IMPORTS

Germany is one of the world's best markets, and the economic opportunities receive political support from a government firmly commited to free trade. However, foreign exporters should be aware of the problems they may encounter in the lucrative German market.

Not surprisingly, various controls and standards are imposed on certain types of goods, including food, live animals, matches containing yellow phosphorus, DDT, and alcohol. The government also requires licenses for goods from particular sources. Bilateral voluntary limits apply to steel imports into the EC from a variety of producers; textiles are regulated by some quotas; and various products from less developed countries – including bananas and rum – are also taxed.

Most exporters will be more concerned with Germany's high standards, as described by the more than 25,000 German Industrial Standards (*Deutsche Industrie Normen* or DIN). Although this system is being relaxed to some extent – largely due to complaints from other industrial producers – it is still one of the most rigorous and extensive in the world. Producers have no legal obligation to meet these standards, but practically speaking, they must do so, since distributors are held responsible by German law for every product that they sell, and Accident Prevention Regulations require that only "safe" equipment can be used in the workplace, as defined by the relevant DIN.

Exporters who want to take advantage of Germany's extensive mail-order industry should be aware that many large direct-mail companies have their own product-testing facilities. These are supervised by 40 government-authorized bodies, who determine whether a product will be marked "GS" – *Geprüfte Sicherheit*, or Tested for Safety. Some may see the GS designation as primarily a legal safeguard, but German consumers also look for reassurance, particularly about foreign products.

In addition to these specialized restrictions, Germany also does have some more standard tariffs and taxes in force. Although there are virtually no tariffs on goods imported from fellow EC members, exporters should research their products' status carefully, since some foodstuffs and agricultural products are taxed. Generally, tariffs are low or non-existent for non-EC members as well.

Although importers must pay the Import Turnover Tax (*Einfuhrumsatzsteuer*), this exactly equals the Value Added Tax (*Mehrwertsteuer*), which must be paid by domestic manufacturers. Excise taxes will be levied against various alcoholic beverages, tobacco, tea, coffee, sugar, salt, perfume, and lighting.

THE LABOR FORCE

Foreign business people may approach the German labor force with both eagerness and trepidation. Eagerness, because the German working population is one of the most skillful, loyal, and conscientious in the industrial world. German productivity continues to increase at 2.5% per year, with Germany able to outperform virtually all competitors in terms of work output per hour.

The trepidation comes because this efficient, productive workforce is both expensive and extremely well-organized in strong, ideologically oriented trade unions. Labor legislation in Germany even goes so far as to specify that office swivel chairs must have five feet – an ergonomic requirement that may pay off in worker health, safety, and productivity, but which also frightens employers from less quality-conscious countries.

The power of the German labor union has been extended via the establishment of worker participation on company boards and in other types of management. German workers enjoy a variety of avenues of influence, including the Factory Council (*Betriebsrat*), the labor court, and the system of *Mitbestimmung*, or worker participation, by which workers have the right to a particular percentage of the seats on supervisory boards of certain companies (50% on the boards of companies with over 2,000 employees; 33% on the boards of companies with over 500 employees).

Although foreigners' initial reaction may be mixed, familiarity with the German system will probably lead ultimately to enthusiasm. Despite the power of labor unions to push for legislation and strong contracts, both workers and managers like to talk about "working together" and "cooperation." As long as they are well compensated and well protected, German workers will richly reward any employer with a level of productivity that is the envy of most of the industrialized world.

Labor relations in Germany are generally peaceful, although the Kohl government has had an ambivalent approach to the union movement over the past decade or so. Nevertheless, the union movement has remained strong, commanding the loyalty of an extremely high percentage of Germany's workers. As in most countries, membership is most loyal in the traditional heavy industries (close to 90%); least union-conscious in the financial services sector (below 30%). Although the largest heavy-industry unions have traditionally been the most militant, the anti-union sentiment of the Kohl government has pushed even the small financial workers' union to become willing to take industrial action.

There are only 17 industrial unions in Germany, all of which belong to the *Deutscher Gewerkschaftsbund* (DGB), a national federation of unions based in Düsseldorf. In addition, there are two civil service unions, a Christian union, and a police union.

Industrial unions negotiate industry-wide contracts every year, meeting with the employers' association for the relevant industry. Although the agreements are legally binding only for the actual unions and employers involved, in fact they generally set the pace for the entire industry.

Although work stoppages – lasting from a few minutes up through several hours – are relatively common in Germany, full-scale strikes are rare. Employers must pay workers during a stoppage, whereas unions must dip into their – relatively small – strike funds in case of a strike. Work stoppages are technically illegal until after the end of the "peace period" of contract negotiations, but unions have found it more effective to conduct stoppages before or even during the talks, in order to remind employers of their militancy and muscle. Sometimes German work stoppages take place right in the negotiations room – a most dramatic reminder of union power.

A less important indicator of union power can be seen in the extensive protections guaranteed by German labor law. For example, in Germany, employers and employees must both contribute to the national health insurance program. Working hours are limited to 40 hours per week, but most blue-collar jobs now require less than 38.5 hours per week, with unions pushing for further reductions. German employers are not allowed to rely too often upon overtime, which must be approved by the Factory Council (elected by workers), and which must be paid at least 25% to 50% above the basic rate.

The Factory Council also has a substantial say in questions of hiring and firing. The Dismaissal Protection Law and the Factory Constitution Law both apply to all companies with more than six employees; they require that the Factory Council be consulted on hiring/firing issues, and that a plan for severance pay must be set up if ten or more workers are laid off. In addition, a fired worker of more than six months' seniority may appeal against his or her dismissal the next day to the labor court (see below).

In addition to labor law, workers have three other forms of legal participation in the system, each of which has inspired skepticism in Germany's unions. The Factory Council – *Betriebsrat* – is elected by the secret ballot of the workers in any company where more than five people are employed. The Council has approval power over working hours, pay methods, vacation schedules, job training, company rules, and hiring. It must also be informed of employment changes, although it does not have approval power over these decisions. Generally, Factory Councils conduct negotiations over such key employment policies as hiring, firing, overtime, vacations, and shift time. Unions often resent them because their priorities tend to go towards preserving jobs, possibly at the expense of working conditions or other union benefits. Union leadership has also accused Factory Council members of "selling out" by becoming a part of management rather than genuine advocates for workers.

For similar reasons, unions are skeptical about *Mitbestimmung*, the system by which workers' representatives get a certain percentage of seats on large company boards. Since the chair – elected by the shareholders – has the final vote in any close contest, unions claim that ultimately their representatives have no power. (The exceptions here are the coal and steel industries, in which a neutral chair acceptable to both sides is chosen.) For their part, business owners have complained that they should not have to give employees such extensive representation, and have often tried to evade the law by changing their company's status.

Labor courts, part of the regular German judiciary, are charged with handling the cases brought by Factory Councils against firings and layoffs. Business observers find that the courts tend to favor the Factory Councils, but decisions that go to final appeal may take three or more years. Thus unions and Factory Councils have found it useful to involve these courts in factory closing issues, as a way of delaying the closure.

HOLIDAYS

The following national public holidays in Germany are days when all shops, stores, and banks are closed except for those at major railway stations:

January 1 –	New Year's Day
Late March/ early April –	Good Friday and Easter Monday
May 1 –	Labor Day
May (date varies) –	Ascension Day (*Himmelfahrt*)
Late May/early June –	Whit Monday
Third Wednesday in November –	*Buß- und Bettag*, Day of Prayer and Repentence
December 25–26 –	First and Second Days of Christmas

Certain parts of Germany also celebrate some religious festivals as public holidays:

January 6 –	Epiphany (celebrated in Baden-Württemberg and Bavaria)
May/June (depending on Easter's date) –	Corpus Christi Day (celebrated in Baden-Württemberg, Hesse, Saarland, North Rhine–Westphalia, Rhineland Palatinate, and Bavaria)
August 15 –	Assumption (celebrated in Saarland and Bavaria)
October 31 –	All Saints Day (celebrated in the

Protestant areas of Schleswig-Holstein and southern Germany)

November 1 – All Saints Day (celebrated in the Catholic areas of Baden-Württemberg, Saarland, North Rhine–Westphalia, Rhineland-Palatinate, and Bavaria)

Rosenmontag, or Carnival Monday, is celebrated in February or March, before Lent. Although it is not an offical holiday, most Rhineland offices are closed at this time.

Non-Germans who are used to vacations of one or two weeks or even less may have to adjust their thinking when it comes to doing business in Germany. Holidays and vacation time are very important to Germans at all levels of the corporate hierarchy, from factory workers to company managers.

Generally, July and August are extremely slow months in Germany, as most employees take their summer holidays, for as long as a month. Some companies, particularly manufacturers, may simply shut down for a month. Christmas and New Year's is likewise a popular holiday time, and many people in business take a whole week off. Although Easter and Whitsun are not quite as popular for holiday time, it may nevertheless be difficult to arrange appointments at that time. It is always wise to check the dates of the holiday periods, as these do vary from district to district.

FOOD

Those who have have grown used to low-fat diets and concerns about cholesterol may need to shift their thinking a bit to enjoy the food they'll find in Germany. Although Germans rarely do business over meals, foreign visitors may be invited to lunch, particularly if an all-day meeting has been scheduled. Germans like what they call *gutbürgerlich* food – simple, well-cooked, meat-and-potato dishes, varying from region to region but everywhere retaining the same basic style.

Pork is one of Germany's most popular meats: served as ham in Westphalia, boiled with *Sauerkraut* in Frankfurt, and roasted with dumplings in Munich.

Sausage (*Wurst*) is another justly famed German specialty, which varies from region to region: white Munich sausages are eaten for breakfast or for a mid-morning snack; long, coiled Nuremberg *Wurst* is roasted for lunch or dinner.

Lamb is also popular as a delicacy, and is readily available in the north. North Sea areas like Hamburg feature fish; the locally-caught trout of Bavaria is also renowned.

Vegetarians will find that most restaurants do have vegetarian dishes on their menu. Chinese cuisine is probably a vegetarian's best choice. Healthy "bio" food, such as raw vegetables and cheese, may be found on some hotel menus. The traveler who is particularly concerned about diet might want to stay at a *Kurhotel*, or health spa.

DRINK

Foreign business travelers may find themselves in the position of ordering drinks for or with German hosts. A general familiarity with German beer, wine, and cider might be useful on such occasions.

German cider is known as *Apfelwein*. It is high in alcohol and is most popular around Frankfurt.

Beer varies a great deal from region to region, so much that different beers have different names. The famous *Weißbier* of Munich is actually made from wheat. In Cologne, *Kölsch* is dry and pale. Franconia's *Rauchbier* has a smoky taste. You will tend to be served the local beer, and the quantity and size of glass varies from region to region.

The most famous German white wine made from the Riesling grape is available from the Rhine, the Mosel, Baden, and Franconia. Particularly good years include Rhine and Mosel: '90, '88, '85, '83, '76, '75 and '71; Baden: '92, '90, '89, '76 and '71; Franconia: '90, '88, '76 and '71. French wines are also readily available in Germany.

For those who don't wish to partake of alcohol, fruit juices and coffee are easily obtainable at any drinking establishment. Whiskey, gin, and other hard spirits are likewise available.

SOURCES OF INFORMATION

Travelers wishing to learn about Germany might check with the commercial section of the local German embassy or consulate. (See "Addresses" section.)

Within Germany, most local government bodies have departments responsible for promoting local economic growth. Germany is divided into regions, or *Länder* and each region's ministry of industry and technology (*Ministerium für Wirtschaft und Technologie*) is charged with overseeing import–export matters. A local chamber of commerce (*Industrie- und Handelskammer*) will provide information about its member businesses. The main reference library of each city (*Bibliothek*) will probably have a commercial section.

A tourist information office (*Verkehrsamt*) can be found at most airports, railway stations, town halls, or key tourist attractions. There a business traveler may get information about transport, places to stay, and local points of interest, as well as help with such mundane matters as where to find a dry cleaner or a drugstore.

EMERGENCIES

In Germany, all emergency calls are free. The following emergency numbers may prove helpful:

Police (*Polizei*) – 110
Fire (*Feuerwehr*) – 112
Ambulance (*Arzt*) – 19292 (in some cities only)

INTERNATIONAL TELEPHONING

The following codes may prove helpful to travelers making international calls while in Germany. Before dialing the country code, a traveler should dial 00, then the international code given below, then the city code (in the United States, the area code), and finally, the number.

Germany is on Central European Time, which is one hour ahead of Greenwich Mean Time, 6 hours ahead of New York's Eastern Standard Time, and 9 hours ahead of Los Angeles and the West Coast. Between March and September, Germany puts clocks ahead one hour. Travelers should check to find out whether their own country's daylight saving schedule corresponds to Germany's.

Each code below is listed with the number of hours that the country is ahead or behind German time, assuming neither country is on daylight savings.

Australia	61 (– 7 to 9 hours)
Austria	43
Belgium	32
Canada	1 (– 4 hours 30 minutes to 9 hours)
Denmark	45
France	33
Greece	30 (+ 1 hour)
Hong Kong	852 (+ 7 hours)
India	91 (+ 4 hours 30 minutes)
Ireland	353 (–1 hour)
Israel	972 (+ 1 hour)
Italy	39
Japan	81 (+ 8 hours)
Netherlands	31
New Zealand	64 (+ 11 hours)
Norway	47
Pakistan	92 (+ 4 hours)
Portugal	351 (– 1 hour)
Singapore	65 (+ 7 hours)
Spain	34
Sweden	46
Switzerland	41
United Kingdom	44 (– 1 hour)
United States	1 (– 6 to 11 hours)

ELECTRICITY

Western visitors bringing electric razors, hair-dryers, electric contact lens sterilizers, and the like should be forewarned that the situation with such appliances may be complicated. Electric current in Germany is 220 AC. Therefore, business travelers from outside Europe planning to use these conveniences may want to purchase adapters or all-purpose converters (which can convert any type of current for use by any appliance).

Business travelers who have brought their own battery chargers, copiers, fax machines, video equipment, computers, electric/

electronic typewriters, and other business-related technology should be particularly careful to bring their own extension cords, adapters, batteries, spare parts, and converters, if necessary. German equivalent equipment may not fit foreign devices: they will probably be geared to the metric system of measurement.

WEIGHTS AND MEASURES

Since the metric system is used throughout Germany, a business traveler's documents should also use this system. Although interpreters will translate into English, they may have difficulties translating into English measurements, so business travelers may wish to carry a small card with a conversion chart (obtainable through most business-supply or stationery stores).

WORKING HOURS

Although official working hours in Germany are 9 to 5, business travelers may expect some variations on this custom. Bankers are probably the type of executive who conform most closely to official hours, not receiving appointments, or admitting to being "in" until 9 a.m. – although many are actually at their desks by 8 a.m. or even earlier.

Company executives in factory towns, on the other hand, are likely to keep factory hours, which begin at 7 a.m. Other German executives may make a practice of being at their desks by 8 a.m. Big-city executives – from Munich, Frankfurt, Düsseldorf, and Hamburg – may come to work slightly later than 8 in order to avoid the factory rush-hour, which peaks just before 7 and is over by 8. In any case, the foreign traveler may well expect to get an 8.30 a.m. appointment from a busy executive.

Although many German managers stay at their desks until 7 p.m., they are unlikely to admit to being in past 5 p.m., when working hours are officially over. They can then use the two hours of quiet to catch up on work that requires periods of uninterrupted time; they can also make international calls before it's lunchtime in New York.

Despite these grueling weekday hours, executives are going along with a growing trend to leave early on Friday afternoons. This trend is specially prevalent in the South.

Under these circumstances, it is understandable that German

executives shy away from overtime or last-minute emergency work sessions. They tend to work methodically for long hours, and then to put their work behind them and go home. Some executives in large cities may stay in town for a drink while the rush hour dies down, but they rarely linger. Since most German managers live in the suburbs they tend to start their homeward journeys early – and to maintain a strong separation between work and private life. They don't expect to take work home, nor to recieve business calls there.

If an emergency call is absolutely required, the foreign traveler should apologize for disturbing the German executive and explain why the urgency was necessary. If a spouse answers, the foreign traveler should apologize to him or her for the intrusion before asking to speak to the colleague.

If business is rarely taken home, it is almost never taken on vacation. Even top executives tend to take a full four weeks in summer plus a week or two in winter – and work is not a part of these holidays. Nor are weekends open to the demands of the office.

Those who work under quite a different ethic should be aware of German feelings on this matter.

DRESSING FOR BUSINESS

German conservative attitudes toward business customs intersect with the rather staid German sense of dress to produce an extremely restrained style of business dress. Men most often wear dark suits, white shirts, and conservative ties. Women likewise wear conservative suits (with skirts, not pants) and white blouses. A German senior executive of either sex will almost never be seen in a light-colored suit or a blazer.

The old-fashioned notion that a gentleman should not be seen in his shirtsleeves is not considered old-fashioned at all in Germany. Even in summer, male executives will wear ties and jackets, although in the hottest weather they may concede to wearing slightly less formal clothes, substituting a blazer or a lighter colored suit for their habitual garments.

GIFTS

Business travelers who are used to presenting hosts and colleagues with lavish presents should restrain themselves in Germany. Any substantial gift will be seen as in poor taste. A small token of appreciation, such as a good pen, might be appropriate for an exceptionally generous host.

NEWS SOURCES

There is a variety of German sources for business news. The leading specialized newspaper is the *Handelsblatt*, a business daily comparable to the *Wall Street Journal* or the London *Financial Times*. However, business travelers interested in the stock market may be more interested in the *Börsenzeitung*, and those looking for news on foreign trade should consult the *Nachrichten für Außenhandel*.

Of course, the German daily newspapers also include business coverage, with the *Frankfurter Allgemeine Zeitung* (*FAZ*) as the most respected for its financial news. It is sold nationwide, so foreign travelers may be sure of finding it throughout Germany. Its daily business section is full of helpful information, and its editorial slant is decidedly pro-business.

Die Welt is another nationally distributed German paper, also featuring a daily business section that is highly respected by the country's executives and managers. Travelers in Munich may prefer *Süddeutsche Zeitung*, which is likewise highly regarded.

News agencies in Germany frequently specialize in economic and business news. The most important is the *Vereinigte Wirtschaftsdienste* (*VWD*), which includes both ticker and screen service as well as publishing various specialized reports each day. Reuters and AP Dow Jones/Telerate, based in London, are available in Germany as well.

German-speaking travelers will want to research the variety of specialized business magazines to find those most useful, but they should be aware that virtually all German executives feel they must keep up with *Der Spiegel*, a kind of German equivalent of *Time* or *Newsweek* or *The Economist* in the UK, coverage. If there is a business-related scandal anywhere in Germany, chances are good the *Der Spiegel* will cover it. *Manager Magazine* is the monthly controlled by *Der Spiegel*, enjoying a similar reputation for its tough business coverage.

Der Platow Brief is available two to three times a week for those looking for specialized stock-market coverage. Middle managers frequently read *Wirtschaftswoche* every week and *Capital* and *Industriemagazine* every month.

For those who prefer to get their news on television and radio, German business coverage is likely to be disappointing. Only major changes in government policy or foreign exchange rates are likely to be covered, and the stock market is rarely given airtime.

ARRIVING AT
THE AIRPORT

3

ARRIVING AT THE AIRPORT

Arriving in Germany is fairly simple: all a traveler really needs is a valid passport and a return ticket. For travelers not holding a European passport, no visa is required for any visit of less than three months.

Here is my passport.
Hier ist mein Paß.
heer isst mine pahss.

I am staying only a few days.
Ich bleibe nur einige Tage.
ikh BLY-beh noor EYE-nee-geh TA-gheh.

... a week
... eine Woche
... INE-neh VO-kheh.

... a month
... einen Monat
... inen MO-naht.

CUSTOMS

Customs in Germany are also fairly simple. Travelers may bring in any item or equipment intended for their personal use. They may bring in a fixed amount of alcohol, perfume, and tobacco duty-free. However, there are two categories under which these items are taxed: those bought in a duty-free shop or in a non-EC European country and those bought in an EC country where tax and duty has already been paid. The chart below gives the regulations.

	Duty-Free or Non-EC	**EC Country**
Alcohol	2 l wine to 22% or 1 l wine over 22% or 2 l table wine	3 l sparking wine to 22% or 1.5 l wine to 22% or 5 l table wine
Tobacco	200 cigarettes or 50 cigars	300 cigarettes or 75 cigars or 150 cigarillos

	or 100 cigarillos or 250g tobacco	or 400g tobacco
Perfume	50g perfume and 0.25 l toilet water	75g perfume and 0.375 l toilet water
Other goods	100g tea or 40g extract 250g coffee or 100g extract goods to the value of 115 DM	200g tea or 60g extract 1,000g coffee or 300g extract goods to the value of 780 DM

RECLAIMING THE VALUE ADDED TAX

The traveler who is taking goods from Germany into another EC country can reclaim the Value Added Tax (VAT) on arrival at the other country's customs, but the traveler must show a signed receipt. Travelers should be sure to get receipts from German customs upon departure, for both EC countries and other countries.

This is just for my personal use.
Das ist nur für meinen persönlichen Bedarf.
Dahss isst noor für MY-nen pehr-ZERN-lee-khen beh-DAHV.

I will not be selling this.
Ich werde das nicht verkaufen.
ikh VEER-deh dahss nikt fair-KOW-fen.

This is a present for my family.
Das ist ein Geschenk für meine Familie.
dahss isst EYE-n geh-SHENK für MY-neh fa-MEE-lee-yeh.

I need this for my business.
Ich brauche das für mein Geschäft.
Ikh BROW-kheh dahss für mine guh-SHEFT.

I bought this at the Duty-Free Shop.
Ich habe das im Taxfreien Geschäft gekauft.
ikh HA-beh dahss imm tahks-FRY-yen guh-SHEFT guh-KOWFT.

I bought this in an EC country.
Ich habe das in einem EG Land gekauft.
ikh HA-beh dahss in EYE-nehm Eh-gheh-lahnt guh-KOWFT.

This is from a non-EC country.
Das ist von einem Nicht EG Land.
dahss isst fohn EYE-nem nihkt Eh-Gheh lahnt.

This is all the alcohol I have.
Das sind alle Spirituosen, die ich habe.
dahss zint AH-leh spee-ree-TUO-zen dee ikh HA-be.

This is just table wine.
Das ist nur Tafelwein.
dahss isst noor TA-fel-vine.

I don't have any more cigarettes.
Ich habe keine Zigaretten mehr.
ikh HA-beh KYE-neh tsig-ah-RET-ten mare.

Here is all my tobacco.
Das sind alle Tabakwaren, die ich habe.
dahss zint AH-leh ta-bahk-VA-ren dee ikh HA-beh.

This is perfume, but that is toilet water.
Das ist Parfüm, aber das ist eau de toilette.
dahss isst par-FUM AH-ber dahss isst oh de toilette.

Can I have a receipt, please?
Ich möchte eine Quittung, bitte.
ikh MERK-teh EYE-neh kvee-toong BIT-te.

MONEY

There are no currency restrictions for business travelers coming into Germany. Travelers may bring in or take out as much currency as they like.

The currency in Germany is called the *Deutschmark* (DM). The mark is divided into 100 *Pfennige* (Pfg). D-Mark notes can be found in the following denominations: 10, 20, 50, 100, 500, and

1,000. Coins can be found in units of 1, 2, 5, 10, and 50 Pfg., as well as for 1, 2, and 5 DM.

Most public telephones in Germany take 50 Pfg pieces and 1, 2, or 5 DM coins. Parking meters accept 10 Pfg. and 1 DM coins. The 2 and 5 DM coins are useful for tipping.

The best place to change money in Germany is at a bank. Many bank branches can be found at international airports and major railway stations, using the official rate of exchange set by the Bundesbank, or state bank. However, because of their location, they are often open outside normal banking hours, and are likely to be available when most travelers arrive. It is also possible to exchange money at a *Wechselstube*, or exchange bureau, as well as at big hotels, at a post office (*Postamt*), or at some travel agencies.

Where can I exchange money?
Wo kann ich Geld umtauschen?
vo kahn ikh gelt OOM-tau-shen?

I need to cash a traveler's check.
Ich möchte einen Reisescheck einlösen.
ikh MERK-teh inen RYE-zeh-shek INE-ler-zen

Can I have some smaller denominations, please?
Können Sie mir eine kleinere Wertung geben?
KERN-nen zee meer EYE-neh KLI-neh-reh VAIR-toong GAY-ben?

Can I have some change, please?
Können Sie mir etwas Wechselgeld geben?
KERN-nen zee meer ET-vahs VEX-sel-gelt GAY-ben?

I need some 10 Pfg. pieces.
Ich brauche einige Zehnpfennigstücke.
ikh BROW-kheh EYE-neh-geh tsayn-FEN-nig-stŭ-keh.

I need some 1 DM pieces.
Ich brauche einige Einmarkstücke.
ikh BROW-kheh EYE-nee-geh INE-mark-stŭ-keh.

May I please have some 2 and 5 DM coins?
Kann ich einige 2-DM und 5-DM Stücke haben?
Kahn ikh eye-nee-geh tsvy Day-M oont fünf Day-M SHTÜ-keh ha-ben?

Credit cards are not as widely used in Germany as in other Western European countries, and may not be as widely accepted. Even large bills are often paid in cash. However, most hotels, large stores, and car rental agencies will accept most major credit cards and Eurocheques, although most small shops will not.

I would like to withdraw money with my American Express card,
Ich möchte gern Geld mit meiner A-E Karte abheben,
ikh MERK-teh GAIRN gelt mit MY-ner ah-eh KAR-teh AHB-heh-ben

and change into German marks.
und in D-Mark umtauschen.
oont in DEH-mark OOM-t' ow-shen.

... my Visa Card.
... VEE-sah Kar-teh.

... my Master Card.
.... MAR-steh Kar-teh.

... my Diners Club Card.
... DYE-ners Club Kar-teh.

Do you accept this card?
Nehmen Sie diese Karte an?
NAY-men zee DEE-seh KAR-teh ahn?

AT THE HOTEL

TAXIS FROM THE AIRPORT

The simplest way of reaching one's hotel is usually by taxi. Interestingly, taxis throughout Germany all look much the same. All are beige or white; most are diesel-engined Mercedes, although there are some Ford Taunuses and Opels.

Excuse me, where can I find a taxi here?
Verzeihung, wo kann ich hier eine Taxe finden?
fair-TSY-oong, vo kahn ikh here EYE-neh TAHK-seh FIN-den?

Can you take me to the ___ Hotel?
Können Sie mich zum Hotel ___ bringen?
KER-nen zee mikh ts' oom ho-TEL ___ BRING-en?

Most taxi drivers do not speak English, so a traveler may have to ask someone to give instructions to the driver.

Do you speak English?
Sprechen Sie englisch?
SPREH-khen zee ENG-lish?

Excuse me, I don't speak much German.
Entschuldigen Sie, ich spreche nicht viel deutsch.
ent-SHOOL-deeg-en zee, ikh SPREH-khe nikht feel doytch.

only a little.
nur ein bißchen.
noor ine BISS-khen.

The address is on the paper.
Die Adresse ist auf diesem Papier.
dee ah-DRES-seh isst owf DEE-sem pa-PEER.

Please tell this driver to take me to the hotel ___ .
Bitte sagen Sie dem Fahrer, daß er mich zum Hotel ___ bringen soll.
BIT-teh ZA-ghen zee dem FA-rer, dass air mikh ts' oom ho-TEL ___ BRING-en zoll.

AT THE HOTEL

Taxi! To the Hotel ___.
Taxi! zum Hotel ___.
TAHK-see! ts' oom ho-TEL ___.

German taxi fares are always metered. Unfortunately, they are also rather expensive, at least DM 3-4 per kilometer. A traveler should make sure to tip the cab driver so that the fare has at least been rounded up to the nearest mark.

How much will it cost to go to the Hotel ___?
Wieviel wird es zum Hotel ___ kosten?
vee-FEEL veerd ess ts' oom ho-TEL ___ KO-sten?

How much do I owe you?
Wieviel schulde ich Ihnen?
vee-FEEL SHOOL-deh ikh EE-nen?

Here you are.
Bitteschön!
BIT-teh-shern!

You're welcome!
Bitteschön!
BIT-teh-shern!

German taxi drivers are used to giving receipts for taxi fares, but foreign travelers must request them. Even a driver who doesn't speak English will understand the request for a receipt, or *Quittung*.

May I have a receipt, please?
Darf ich bitte eine Quittung haben?
darf ikh BIT-teh EYE-neh KVEET-toong HA-ben?

Thank you very much.
Vielen Dank.
FEE-len dahnk.

Thank you for the pleasant ride.
Vielen Dank für die angenehme Fahrt.
FEE-len dahnk fur dee ahn-guh-nay-meh fahrt.

CHOOSING A HOTEL

Most hotels in the former Federal German Republic (West Germany) are of extremely high quality. Hotels in the former German Democratic Republic (East Germany) are not likely to be of comparable quality, although they do tend to have higher standards and better service than elsewhere in Eastern Europe.

Business in West Berlin and West Germany, however, has been largely reliant on trade fairs, sales conferences, and management meetings, necessitating an excellent system of business accommodation. Both chains and family-run hotels—of which there are many in Germany—pride themselves on their high standards of comfort and cleanliness. Even if travelers find themselves staying in a small, local guesthouse, they may be reasonably certain of finding pleasant, clean, and comfortable rooms.

International hotel chains, such as Hilton, Ramada, Pullman, Intercontinental, and Holiday Inn, are expanding their luxury and high-end service in the form of modern skyscrapers with fairly standardized facilities.

I have always had good service from your company.
Ich habe immer guten Service von Ihrer Firma bekommen.
ikh HA-beh IMM-er GOO-ten Zair-VEES fohn EE-rer feer-ma beh-KO-men.

I have stayed in your hotels before.
Ich war schon mehrmals in Ihren Hotels.
Ikh var shohn MARE-mahlz in EE-ren ho-TELS.

I am always happy to stay in your hotel.
Ich bleibe immer gern in Ihrem Hotel.
Ikh BLEYE-beh imm-er gairn in EE-rem ho-TEL.

On the other hand, travelers to Germany have the option of private hotels reflecting local style, frequently run by families who take pride in their distinctive furnishings and decor. A private hotel, for example, might feature a featherbed, or comforter (*Federbett*), rather than sheets and blankets, or a restaurant with alcove seating.

Is this your own hotel?
Gehört Ihnen dieses Hotel?
geh-hurt EE-nen DEE-zess ho-TEL?

The furnishings are beautiful.
Die Möbel sind sehr schön.
dee MER-bel zint zehr shern.

What a charming restaurant!
Es ist ein reizendes Restaurant!
ess isst ine RYE-tsen-dess res-tau-RAHNT!

What a comfortable bed!
Was für ein komfortables Bett!
vahss fur ine kom-for-TA-bless bet!

This is a lovely room.
Es ist ein wunderschönes Zimmer!
ess isst ine voon-dehr-SHERN-ess TZIM-mer!

Hotels in Germany are not officially graded, although they are rated by Varta. The staff of this influential guide keeps up with regular inspections of the hotels that it rates. Other guides may also give ratings, but these are not so well-regarded as Varta's. In addition, hotels often rate themselves; travelers should be aware that these star-rating are not official:

1 and 2 stars	–	Guesthouse accommodation; used mainly by tourists
3 and 4 stars	–	Small hotels; medium price range with facilities to match
5 stars	–	First-class facilities for business travelers
Luxury	–	Supposedly offering the highest standards of comfort and the most elaborate facilities

What rating does this hotel have?
Welcher Klasse ist dieses Hotel?
VEL-kheh KLA-seh isst DEE-zess ho-TEL?

I am looking for a five-star hotel.
Ich suche nach einem Fünf-Sterne-Hotel.
ikh ZOO-keh nahkh EYE-nem fünf SHTEHR-neh ho-TEL.

Is this a luxury hotel?
Ist dies ein Luxushotel?
isst DEE-ss ine LOOK-susho-TEL?

As they are not rated, hotels in Germany are not officially categorized, either. The following chart should help travelers assess the various facilities they might expect to find:

Hotel	At least 20 rooms, most with bathroom
Hotel Garni	Provides breakfast and snacks; no restaurant
Hotelpension	Provides meals for guests only; limited service
Fremdenheim	Also a pension, but with even more limited services
Gasthof	Mainly for tourists (as opposed to business travelers); bedrooms, usually without private baths
Gasthaus	Mainly for tourists; bedrooms, usually without private baths
Kurhotel	Provides special diets and medical services; usually found only in spas and resorts
Appartementhotel	Self-catering suites with hotel facilities

Does this rate include meals?
Sind in diesem Preis Mahlzeiten einbegriffen?
zint in DEE-zem price MAHL-tsite-ten INE-beh-grif-fen?

Which meals are included?
Welche Mahlzeiten sind einbegriffen?
VEL-kheh MAHL-tsite-en zint INE-beh-grif-fen?

I don't want my meals here; is the rate lower?
Ich möchte hier keine Mahlzeiten einnehmen; ist der Preis dann niedriger?
ikh MERK-teh here KYE-neh MAHL-tsite-ten INE-neh-men; isst dehr price dahn KNEE-drig-gher?

RESERVING A ROOM

Once travelers arrive at their hotels, they are likely to find at least some employees who speak English. The range of fluency, however, is likely to vary, depending on the size of the hotel.

Do you speak English?
Sprechen Sie englisch?
SPREH-khen zee ENG-lish?

I'm sorry, I don't speak German well.
Es tut mir leid, ich spreche nicht gut deutsch.
ess toot meer lite, ikh SPREH-kheh nikht goot doytch.

Does anyone speak English?
Gibt es hier jemanden der englisch spricht?
ghibt ess here YAY-mahn-den dehr ENG-lish SPRIKht?

Reservations at German hotels should definitely be made well ahead of time, particularly if a traveler is arriving in a city during a trade fair. Most privately owned hotels belong to some kind of international service or network through which reservations can be made. However, a traveler can also contact a local tourist office, which can make reservations by telephone or fax or through a travel agency. During a trade fair, the use of bed-and-breakfasts and guesthouses is common.

I need a hotel reservation, please.
Ich brauche eine Hotelreservation, bitte.
ikh BROW-kheh EYE-neh ho-TEL-reh-zair-vahts'YOHN, BIT-eh.

Can you help me make a hotel reservation?
Können Sie mir bei der Hotelreservierung helfen?
KER-nen zee meer by dehr ho-TEL-reh-zair-vee-ROONG
HELL-fen?

I would like to stay for one day.
Ich möchte einen Tag bleiben.
ikh MERK-teh EYE-nen takh BLY-bin.

... two days.
... zwei Tage.
... ts'vye TA-geh.

... three days.
... drei Tage.
... dry TA-geh.

... four days.
... vier Tage.
...feer TA-geh.

... five days.
... fünf Tage.
...fünf TA-geh.

... for a week.
... eine Woche.
... EYE-neh VO-kheh.

... for two weeks.
... für zwei Wochen.
...für ts'vye VO-khen.

... until Monday.
... bis Montag.
... bis mohn-tahk.

... until Tuesday.
... bis Dienstag.
... biss deens-tahk.

... Wednesday.
... Mittwoch.
... mitt-vohk.

... Thursday.
... Donnerstag.
... dun-ners-tahk.

... Friday.
... Freitag.
... FRY-tahk.

... Saturday.
... Sonnabend.
... zon-na-bent.

... Sunday.
... Sonntag.
... ZOHN-tahk.

Corporate Rates

Frequently, corporate rates are available, as are discounts for visits lasting three days or longer. Travelers should always ask about discounts for these occasions, as for groups of 10 of more people, who may receive a 30% reduction at some hotels. In addition, weekend rates are lower than usual, as are July and August prices (except in such tourist areas as the Rhineland and Bavaria).

Is there a discount?
Gibt es einen Rabatt?
ghibt ess EYE-nen ra-BAHT?

I will be staying for more than three days.
Ich bleibe mehr als drei Tage.
ikh BLY-beh mair ahlz dry TA-geh.

There are more than ten people in our group.
In unsere Gruppe sind mehr als zehn Leute.
in OON-seh-rer GROO-peh zint mair ahlz tsehn LOY-teh.

Is there a corporate rate?
Gibt es einen Korporationspreis?
ghibt ess EYE-nen kor-po-rahts-YOHNS-price?

I have a reservation.
Ich habe eine Reservierung.
ikh HA-beh EYE-neh reh-zair-VEE-roong.

My reservation has been confirmed.
Meine Reservierung ist bestätigt.
MINE-neh reh-zair-VEE-roong isst beh-SHTEH-tigt.

I want a single room.
Ich möchte ein Einzelzimmer.
ikh MERK-teh ine INE-tzel-tzim-mer.

I want a double room.
Ich möchte ein Doppelzimmer.
ikh MERK-teh ine DOHP-pel-tzim-mer.

What are your daily rates?
Wie sind Ihre Tagespreise?
vie zint EE-reh TAH-ghes-pry-zeh?

... weekly rates?
... Wochenpreise?
... VO-khen-PRY-zeh?

I want a deluxe room.
Ich möchte ein Luxuszimmer.
ikh MERK-teh ine looksus-ZIM-mer.

I want a suite.
Ich möchte eine Suite.
ikh MERK-teh EYE-neh sweet.

ROOMS AND FACILITIES

In luxury hotels, business travelers can expect private bathrooms, with both bath and shower. They can also expect color television sets, minibars, and direct-dial telephones for long-distance and international calls.

Does this room have a bathtub?
Hat dieses Zimmer eine Badewanne?
hat DEE-zess TSIM-mer EYE-neh BA-deh-va-neh?

I would like a room with a bathtub, please.
Ich hätte gern ein Zimmer mit Badewanne.
ikh HET-teh GEHR-n ine TSIM-mer mit BA-de-wa-neh.

... with a shower.
... mit Dusche.
... mit DOO-sheh.

Can I have more towels, please?
Kann ich bitte noch mehr Handtücher haben?
kahn ikh BIT-eh nohkh mehr HANT-tukher HA-ben?

Can you show me how to work the television set?
Können Sie mir zeigen, wie der Fernseher funktioniert?
KER-nen zee meer TSY-ghen vee dehr fern-SEH-er
foonk-ts'yohn-EERT?

Is there an English language program?
Gibt es ein Programm in englischer Sprache?
ghibt ess ine pro-grahm in ENG-lee-sher spra-kheh?

Can you show me how to make a long-distance call?
Können Sie mir zeigen, wie man ein Ferngespräch macht?
KER-nen zee meer TSY-ghen vee mahn ine fern-geh-sprehk makht?

How do I call America?
Wie rufe ich Amerika an?
vee ROOFe ikh ah-MEH-ree-ka ahn?

How do I call England?
Wie kann ich England anrufen?
vee kahn ikh ENG-lahnt AHN-roo-fen?

How can I call Canada?
Wie kann ich Kanada anrufen?
vee kahn ikh KA-na-da AHN-roo-fen?

How do I call Japan?
Wie rufe ich Japan an?
vee ROO-feh ikh ya-PAHN ahn?

How does the minibar work?
Wie funktioniert die Minibar?
vee foonk-ts'yohn-EERT dee MEE-nee-bar?

Where is the price list?
Wo ist die Preisliste?
vo isst dee PRICE-lis-teh?

Most hotel rooms in Germany do not come equipped with hair dryers or irons, but these are usually available at the front desk.

The German voltage of 220 AC does not usually agree with American appliances, so foreign travelers may need a transformer. American and English travelers will need an adapter for any of their own appliances.

Can I borrow a hair dryer, please?
Kann ich bitte einen Haartrockner leihen?
kahn ikh BIT-teh EYE-nen HAHR-truch-nehr LYE-hen?

Excuse me, I would like to borrow an iron.
Entschuldigen Sie bitte, ich hätte gern ein Bügeleisen geliehen.
ent-SHOOL-dee-ghen zee BIT-teh, ikh HET-eh gairn ine BU-gel-eye-zen geh-LEE-hen.

Do you have a transformer?
Haben Sie einen Transformator?
HA-ben zee EYE-nen trahns-FOR-ma-tor?

Do you have an adapter?
Haben Sie einen Adapter?
HA-ben zee EYE-nen ah-DAHP-ter?

Excuse me, how can I use this appliance in my hotel room?
Verzeihung, wie kann ich dieses Gerät in meinem Hotelzimmer benutzen?
fair-TSY-hoong, vee kahn ikh DEEzess geh-REHT in MY-nem ho-TEL-tzim-mer beh-NOOT-zen?

FOOD AND DRINK

Most hotel rooms will not have facilities for making tea or coffee, but these can usually be obtained in the coffee shop or the lobby. Most hotels serve a continental breakfast of bread rolls, croissants, bread, butter, jam, cheese and cold meat.

A buffet might have a cooked breakfast, more common in large international hotels. You should be offered fruit juice and tea, coffee, or hot chocolate. Some hotels have a "bio" section of healthy raw ingredients.

Where can I get a cup of coffee?
Wo kann ich eine Tasse Kaffee bekommen?
vo kahn ikh EYE-neh TA-seh KA-feh beh-KO-men?

Where can I get a cup of tea?
Wo kann ich eine Tasse Tee bekommen?
vo kahn ikh INE-neh TA-seh tay beh-KO-men?

Do you have decaffeinated coffee?
Haben Sie kaffeinfreien Kaffee?
HA-ben zee ka-fine-FRY-en KA-feh?

Do you have decaffeinated tea?
Haben Sie kaffeinfreien Tee?
HA-ben zee ka-fine-FRY-en tay?

What time is breakfast served?
Wann wird das Frühstück serviert?
van veert dahss FRÜH -stück zehr-VEERT?

Where is breakfast served?
Wo wird das Frühstück serviert?
vo veert dahss FRÜH-stück zehr-VEERT?

What do you serve for breakfast?
Was servieren Sie zum Frühstück?
Vass zehr-VEE-ren zee tsoom FRÜH-stück?

Can you help me?
Können Sie mir helfen?
KER-nen zee meer HEL-fen?

I am on a low-salt diet. Can you help me?
Ich bin an einer niedrigen Salz Diät. Können Sie mir helfen?
ikh bin ahn EYE-ner NEED-reeg-en zahlz DEE-yet.
KER-nen zee meer HEL-fen?

I am on a low-fat diet.
Ich bin an einer niedrigen Fett Diät.
ikh bin ahn EYE-ner NEED-reeg-en fett DEE-yet.

Most international hotel chains will have a full complement of restaurants. Smaller hotels and guesthouses may not, but the owners can often recommend good local establishments.

Where are the restaurants near here?
Wo befinden sich Restaurants hier in der Nähe?
vo beh-FIN-den zickh res-tau-RAHNTS here in dehr NAY-heh?

I want to make reservation for dinner.
Ich möchte eine Reservierung zum Abendessen machen.
ikh MERK-teh EYE-neh reh-sehr-VEE-rung tsoom AH-bent-es-sen MAHK-en.

There will be ____ people in our party.
Wir sind ____ Leute in unserer Gruppe.
veer zint ____ loy-teh in OON-ser-er GROO-peh.

Do you have a menu in English?
Haben Sie eine Speisekarte in englisch?
HA-ben zee EYE-neh SHPY-zeh-KAR-teh inn ENG-lish?

When do you serve lunch?
Wann wird das Mittagessen serviert?
Wahn veert dahss MEE-takh-ESS-en zehr-VEERT?

What time does dinner begin?
Um wieviel Uhr beginnt das Abendessen?
oom vee-FEEL oor beh-GHINT dahss AH-bent-ess-en?

How late do you serve dinner?
Bis wann wird das Abendessen serviert?
bis WAHN veert dahss AH-bent-ess-en zehr-VEERT?

AT THE HOTEL

Can you recommend a good restaurant for dinner?
Können Sie ein gutes Restaurant zum Abendessen vorschlagen?
KER-nen zee ine GOO-tess res-tau-RAHNT tsoom AH-bent-es-sen for-shla-ghen?

Can you help me make a reservation?
Können Sie mir helfen, eine Reservation zu machen?
KER-nen zee meer HEL-fen, EYE-neh reh-zehr-va-TS'YOHN tsoo MA-khen?

Although German hotels do sell liquor, it is generally cheaper to buy drinks at bars or inns. However, wine in German hotels is of comparable price to other establishments.

I am having a small reception here.
Ich habe hier einen kleinen Empfang.
ikh HA-beh here EYE-nen KLY-nen EMP-fahng.

Can I arrange for drinks?
Kann ich für Getränke arrangieren?
kahn ikh für geh-TRENK-eh ah-rahn-JEER-en?

I would like to order a bottle of wine, please.
Ich hätte gerne eine Flasche Wein, bitte.
ikh HET-eh GAIR-neh EYE-neh FLAH-sheh vine, BIT-teh.

... red wine.	... a dry wine
... Rotwein.	**... einen trockenen Wein.**
... ROHT-vine.	*... EYE-nen TRO-ken-en vine.*
... white wine.	... your best local wine.
... Weißwein.	**... Ihren besten, hiesigen Wein.**
... VICE-vine.	*... EE-ren BES-ten HEE-seeg-en vine.*

... a French wine, please.
... einen französischen Wein, bitte.
... Eye-nen frahn-tser-see-shen vine, BIT-teh.

BUSINESS SERVICES

The better German hotels will certainly be equipped with all the facilities that a business traveler might need: telex, photocopying facilities, faxes, and excellent long-distance telephone service. Business travelers who want word-processing, translating, secretarial services, and printing can usually arrange these through their hotel.

Where is your telex?
Wo ist Ihr Telex?
vo isst eer TEH-lex?

I need to have something copied.
Ich muss etwas kopieren lassen.
ikh mooss ET-vahss ko-PEE-ren LAHS-sen.

Where can I get papers copied?
Wo kann ich Unterlagen kopieren lassen?
vo kahn ikh OON-tehr-lah-ghen ko-PEE-ren LAHS-sen?

Do you have a fax machine?
Haben Sie eine Faxmaschine?
HA-ben zee EYE-neh fahx-ma-SHEE-neh?

Can I receive faxes here?
Kann ich Faxe hier bekommen?
kahn ikh FAHX-eh here beh-KO-men?

What is the number for your fax?
Wie ist Ihre Faxnummer?
vee isst EE-reh FAHX-noo-mer?

How much do you charge to send a fax?
Wieviel verlangen Sie, um ein Fax zu schicken?
vee-FEEL fair-LAHNG-en zee oom INE fahx tsoo SHIH-ken?

How much do you charge to receive a fax?
Wieviel verlangen Sie, wenn Sie ein Fax erhalten?
vee-FEEL fair-LAHNG-en zee, venn zee INE fahx ehr-HAHL-ten?

AT THE HOTEL

How do I make a long-distance call?
Wie führe ich ein Ferngespräch?
vee FÜ-reh ikh ine FERN-geh-sprake?

Can I arrange for a translator?
Kann ich für einen Dolmetscher arrangieren?
kahn ikh für EYE-nen DOHL-met-sher ah-rahn-JEE-ren?

I need a secretary; do you have one available?
Ich brauche eine Sekretärin, haben Sie eine zur Verfügung?
*ikh BROW-keh EYE-ne sek-ree-TEHR-inn; HA-ben zee EYE-neh
tsoor fehr-FÜ-goong?*

I need a secretary who speaks English.
Ich brauche eine Sekretärin, die englisch spricht.
*ikh BROW-keh EYE-neh sek-ree-TEHR-inn dee EHNG-lish
shprikht.*

How do I hire a typist?
Wie kann ich eine Schreibmaschinenkraft einstellen?
vee kahn ikh EYE-neh shryb-ma-SHEE-nen-krahft INE-shtel-len?

I must find someone who can take dictation.
Ich muß jemanden finden, der Diktat aufnehmen kann.
ikh moose YAY-mahn-den FIN-den dehr dik-TAHT owf-neh-men kahn.

I have several documents to print; can you help me?
Ich muß mehrere Dokumente drucken, können Sie mir helfen?
*ikh moose MEH-reh-reh doh-ku-MEN-te DROO-ken; KERN-nen
zee meer HEL-fen?*

What kind of computer facilities do you have?
Welche Art von Computermöglichkeiten haben Sie?
VEL-kheh art fohn com-POO-ter-MERK-lick-eye-ten HA-ben zee?

How can I convert my disks to your system?
Wie kann ich meine Disketten für Ihr System umformatieren?
*vee kahn ikh MY-neh dees-ket-tehn für eer sis-TEM
oom-FOR-MAH-tee-rehn?*

Can I use the computer myself?
Kann ich den Computer selbst benutzen?
kahn ikh den com-POO-ter zelbst beh-NU-tsen?

How much will you charge for me to use the computer?
Was schulde ich Ihnen für die Benutzung des Computers?
Vahs SHOOL-deh ikh EE-nen für dee beh-NOOT-soong dess com-POO-ters?

CONFERENCE FACILITIES

The larger German hotels will have even more elaborate business facilities. Most casual discussions can be held in hotel lobbies; conference rooms are frequently available for more confidential talks. When they are available, conference rooms come equipped with microphones, screens, overhead projectors, and flip charts. The traveler who is willing to pay extra may arrange closed-circuit television transmission, simultaneous interpretation, and other more sophisticated services. Travelers should remember that European videocassettes and videocassette recorders differ from American or Canadian equipment; they may need to bring their own VCRs if they plan to make presentations. If German colleagues wish to make video presentations, the hotel may be able to help find the proper equipment.

Do you have a conference room?
Haben Sie ein Konferenzzimmer?
HA-ben zee ine kohn-fehr-RENTStsim-mer?

How much do you charge for it?
Was nehmen Sie dafür?
vahss NEH-men zee da-für?

Can you serve us coffee there?
Können Sie uns dort Kaffee servieren?
KER-nen zee oonts dort ka-FEH sehr-VEE-ren?

Can you serve us drinks there?
Können Sie uns dort Getränke servieren?
KER-nen zee oonts dort geh-TREN-keh sehr-VEE-ren?

How much will it cost?
Wieviel wird es kosten?
vee-FEEL veert ess KO-sten?

Do you have a pointer?
Haben Sie ein Messgerät?
HA-ben zee ine MESS-geh-ret?

Where is the overhead projector?
Wo ist die Vorführmaschine?
vo isst dee for-FÜR-ma-SHEEN-eh?

Can you show me how it works?
Können Sie mir zeigen, wie das Gerät funktioniert?
*KERN-nen zee meer ZY-ghen vee dahss GEH-ret
foonk-s'yo-NEERT?*

Can I rent a VCR?
Kann ich einen Video Rekorder mieten?
kahn ikh EYE-nen VEE-deh-oh-recorder meeh-tehn?

Where can I plug in my VCR?
Wo kann ich meinen Videorekorder anschließen?
vo kahn ikh MY-nen VEE-deh-oh-re-corder AHN-shlee-sen?

Do you have an adapter?
Haben Sie einen Adapter?
HA-ben zee EYE-nen ah-DAHP-ter?

I need a transformer.
Ich brauche einen Transformater.
ikh BROW-kheh EYE-nen trans-for-MA-tor.

Where is the screen?
Wo ist die Leinwand?
vo isst dee line-vahnt?

How can I show slides in here?
Wie kann ich hier Dias zeigen?
vee kahn ikh here DEE-ahs TSY-ghen?

How do I turn out the lights?
Wie schalte ich das Licht aus?
vee SHALL-teh ikh dahss LICK-t owss?

Can I arrange for closed-circuit television?
Besteht die Möglichkeit für innerbetriebliches Fernsehen?
beh-shtayt dee merklikh-kait für INN-er-beh-treeb-likh-ehs
FAIRN-zay-n?

How much will it be?
Wieviel wird das kosten?
vee-FEEL veert das KOH-sten?

Can you find us a simultaneous interpreter?
Können Sie uns einen gleichzeitigen Dolmetscher finden?
KER-nen zee oons EYE-nen glike-TSITE-tee-ghen DOHL-met-sher
FIN-den?

What will he/she charge?
Was wird er/sie verlangen?
vahss veert ehr/zee fehr-LAHNG-en?

TIPPING

German hotel personnel are almost invariably courteous and help-ful, whether or not they speak English. Foreign travelers who are respectful and pleasant in return will find their courtesy well rewarded.

It is customary to tip porters DM 1–2 per bag or per service. The head porter (*Chef-Portier*) may go out of his way to do you a special service, in which case he should also be tipped. This is in addition to the 10% service charge (*Bedienung*) that most hotels add to their bills.

Is this the service charge?
Ist das die Bezahlung für die Bedienung?
isst dahss dee beh-TSA-loong für dee beh-DEE-noong?

This is for your trouble.
Für Ihre Mühe.
Für EE-reh MU-heh.

Thanks for your help!
Vielen Dank für Ihre Hilfe!
FEE-len dahnk für EE-reh HIL-feh!

You are very kind.
Sie sind sehr freundlich.
zee sint sehr FROYND-lickh.

You have made my stay here very pleasant.
Sie haben meinen Aufenthalt hier sehr angenehm gemacht.
zee HA-ben MY-nen OW-fen-hahlt here zehr AHN-gheh-name geh-MAHKT.

TELEPHONES, FAXES, MAIL, AND COURIERS

5

TELEPHONES

International and local phone services in Germany are very good. The national phone service is operated by the German Post Office. Numbers range from three to eight digits, in addition to a long-distance code. These codes are usually listed by place name in the telephone directory with a full list of national and international codes available in AVON, a booklet of codes (*Vorwahlnummern*).

What is your telephone number?
Wie ist Ihre Telefonnummer?
vee isst EE-reh teh-leh-FOHN-noo-mer?

What is the telephone number of this hotel?
Wie ist die Telefonnummer dieses Hotels?
vee isst dee teh-leh-FOHN-noo-mer DEE-zess ho-TELS?

What is the code for this city?
Wie ist die Vorwahl dieser Stadt?
vee isst dee FOR-vahl DEE-zer shtat?

Do you have the code book?
Haben Sie ein Vorwahlbuch?
HA-ben zee ine FOR-vahl-bookh?

I would like to make an international call.
Ich möchte einen internationalen Anruf machen.
ikh MERK-teh EYE-nen in-tehr-nah-ts' yo-NA-len AHN-roof MA-khen.

Please, what code do I dial for __?
Bitte, welche Vorwahl wähle ich für __?
BIT-teh, VEL-kheh FOR-vahl VAY-leh ikh für __?

Long-distance calls are discounted between 6 p.m. and 8 a.m., Monday to Friday, as well as throughout the entire weekend. Rates are calculated by 12-second units during prime time and by 16-second units during cheap-rate time for long-distance calls; local calls are not timed. Within Germany, there are three charging "zones": up to 50 km/30 miles; up to 100 km/62 miles; and over 100 km, which includes international calls as well as calls from the former West Germany to Berlin and the former East Germany.

Both local and long-distance calls can usually be made directly from the hotel room phone. Travelers can also use pay phone booths located throughout the city for a minimum of 50 Pfg.

Where can I make a phone call?
Wo kann ich telefonieren?
vo kahn ikh teh-leh-fo-NEE-ren?

Where can I get change?
Wo kann ich Kleingeld bekommen?
vo kahn ikhh KLINE-gelt beh-KO-men?

Can you give me change?
Können Sie mir Kleingeld geben?
KER-nen zee meer KLINE-gelt GEH-ben?

I need some 50-pfennig pieces for the phone.
Ich brauche einige Fünfzigpfennigstücke für das Telefon.
*ikh BROW-kheh EYE-nee-geh FŮNF-tsig FEN-nig-stů-keh fůr
dahss teh-leh-FOHN.*

Public booths for local or German long-distance calls are painted yellow and labeled *Telefon* or *Fernsprecher*. It is also possible to reverse charges. In addition, Germany has some numbers labeled "0130," which indicates that callers pay only the local rate, with the call recipient bearing the rest of the price. Many car-rental companies and hotels offer this service.

International calls are made from booths marked with a green sign labeled *Inlands- und Auslandsgespräche.*

I'd like to make a long-distance call.
Ich möchte gerne ein Ferngespräch machen.
ikh MERK-teh GAIR-neh ine FAIRN-geh-sprekh MA-khen.

Can I call long-distance from this phone?
Kann ich ein Ferngespräch von diesem Telefon machen?
*kahn ikh ine FAIRN-geh-spreckh fohn DEE-sem teh-leh-FOHN
MA-khen?*

Where can I make a long-distance call?
Wo kann ich ein Ferngespräch machen?
vo kahn ikh ine FAIRN-geh-spreckh MA-khen?

Can you help me make an international call?
**Können Sie mir helfen, ein internationales Gespräch zu
machen?**
*KER-nen zee meer HEL-fen ine in-ter-na-ts'yo-NA-less
geh-spreckh tsoo MA-khen?*

I'd like to reverse the charges, please.
Ich möchte ein gebürenfreies Gespräch machen, bitte.
*ikh MERK-teh ine geh-BŮ-ren-FRY-es geh-SPREYKH
MA-khen BIT-teh*

Formerly, no calls could be received at public booths, but now,
those labeled *Anrufbares Telefon* and marked with a red sign can
receive calls and are identified with a number. These booths are
frequently located at railway stations.

Directory assistance within Germany can be reached through
1188, or, in smaller towns, 01188. International long-distance can
be reached through 00118.

Can you call me back?
Können Sie mich zurückrufen?
KER-nen zee mikh tsoo-RŮK-roo-fen?

The number is ___.
Die Nummer ist ___.
dee NOO-mer isst ___.

I'm in a telephone booth.
Ich bin in einer Telefonzelle.
ikh bin in EYE-ner teh-leh-FOHN-tsel-ler.

When can I call you back?
Wann kann ich Sie zurückrufen?
vahn kahn ikh zee tsoo-RŮK-roo-fen?

Can you help me find this number?
Können Sie mir helfen, diese Nummer zu finden?
KER-nen zee meer HEL-fen DEE-seh NOO-mer tsoo FIN-den?

I need the number of Mr. ___ , of Mrs. ___ .
Ich brauche die Nummer von Herrn ___ ; von Frau ___ .
ikh BROW-kheh dee NOO-mer fon hairn ___ ; fon Frau ___ .

I need the number of the ___ Company.
Ich brauche die Nummer der Firma ___ .
ikh BROW-kheh dee NOO-mer dehr FEER-ma ___ .

I believe the address is ___ .
Ich glaube, die Adresse ist ___ .
ikh GLOW-beh dee ah-DREH-seh isst ___ .

I do not have the address.
Ich habe die Adresse nicht.
ikh HA-beh dee ah-DREH-seh nihkt.

To reach an operator for help with a local call, dial 101; for help with an international call, dial 0010.

Operator, can you help me place this call?
Operator, können Sie mir mit diesem Anruf helfen?
O-peh-ra-TOR, KER-nen zee meer mit DEE-zem AHN-roof HEL-fen?

Please dial this local number for me.
Bitte wählen Sie diese Ortsnummer für mich.
BIT-teh VAY-len zee DEE-zeh ORTS-noo-mer für mikh.

I have a long-distance call to make within Germany;
the number is ___ .
Ich möchte ein Ferngespräch innerhalb Deutschlands führen;
die Nummer ist ___ .

ikh MERK-teh ine FAIRN-geh-spreckh IN-ner-halp
DOYTSCH-lahnts FÜH-ren;
dee NOO-mer isst ____ .

Can you dial this international number for me, please?
Können Sie diese internationale Nummer für mich wählen?
KERN-nen zee DEE-seh IN-tehr-nahts' yo-NAH-le NOO-mer für
mikh VAY-len?

In English, please.
Auf englisch, bitte.
owf ENG-lish, BIT-teh.

I'm sorry, I don't speak much German.
Es tut mir leid, ich spreche nicht viel deutsch.
ess toot meer lite, ikh SPREH-kheh nihkt feel doytsh.

How long must I wait?
Wie lange muß ich warten?
vee LAHN-geh moose ikh VAHR-ten?

It is very urgent.
Es ist sehr dringend.
ess isst zehr DREEN-ghend.

Generally, hotels will bill both local and long-distance phone charges to the room from which they were made. Travelers should receive a separate listing for phone service on their bills. Like most services, phone connection is more expensive when purchased through the hotel.

Where do I pay for this call?
Wo kann ich für diesen Anruf bezahlen?
vo kahn ikh für DEE-zen AHN-roof beh-TSA-len?

When must I pay?
Wann muß ich bezahlen?
vahn moose ikh beh-TSA-len?

How much did my telephone call cost?
Was hat mein Telefonanruf gekostet?
vahss haht mine teh-leh-FOHN-ahn-roof geh-KO-stet?

As with most things in Germany, formality and courtesy are appreciated in phone manners. Although most Germans speak some English, particularly when they work for companies doing business with foreigners, a few German words show respect for the host country.

May I have your telephone number?
Darf ich Ihre Telefonnummer haben?
darf ikh EE-reh teh-leh-FOHN-noo-mer HA-ben?

Is your number on this card?
Ist Ihre Nummer auf dieser Karte?
isst EE-reh NOO-mer auf DEE-zer KAR-teh?

Can I speak with (Mr.) (Mrs.) (Miss.) ——.
Kann ich mit Herrn (Frau) —— sprechen?
kahn ikh mit hern (frau) —— SPREH-khen?

Can you call him (her) to the phone?
Können Sie ihn (sie) bitte an den Apparat holen?
KERN-en zee ine (zee) BIT-teh ahn dehn ahp-ah-RAHTHOH-len?

May I leave a message?
Kann ich eine Nachricht hinterlassen?
kahn ikh EYE-neh NAKH-rikht HIN-tehr-la-sen?

It's very important.
Es ist sehr wichtig.
ess isst zehr VIKH-tig.

FAXES AND TELEXES

Telexes are easily available in Germany. They can be found at a city's main railway station and at its post offices, as well as at hotels, conference centers, and most trade fairs. As everywhere in the industrialized world, the use of faxes is increasing rapidly, so that by now, virtually every location equipped with a telex is likely to have a fax machine as well – or at least be able to direct the traveler to the nearest fax.

Where can I send a telex?
Wo kann ich ein Telex schicken?
vo kahn ikh ine TEH-lex SHICK-en?

Here is the number.
Hier ist die Nummer.
here isst dee NOO-mer.

Here is the message.
Hier ist die Nachricht.
here isst dee NAHKH-rihkt.

How much will it cost?
Wieviel wird es kosten?
vee-FEEL veert ess KO-sten?

When will it arrive?
Wann wird es ankommen?
vahn veert ess AHN-ko-men?

Can I have a receipt?
Kann ich eine Quittung haben?
kahn ikh EYE-neh KVEET-toong HA-ben?

Can I have a confirmation form?
Kann ich eine Bestätigung haben?
kahn ikh EYE-neh beh-SHTAY-tee-goong HA-ben?

Can you help me with this form?
Können Sie mir mit diesem Formular helfen?
KER-nen zee meer mitt DEE-zem for-moo-LAR HEL-fen?

I thank you for your help.
Ich danke Ihren für Ihre Hilfe.
ikh DAHN-keh EE-nen für EE-reh HIL-feh.

Where can I send a fax?
Wo kann ich ein Fax schicken?
vo kahn ikh ine fahx SHICK-en?

Can you help me with this cover sheet?
Können Sie mir mit diesem Deckblatt helfen?
KER-nen zee meer mitt DEE-zem DECK-blatt HEL-fen?

How much does it cost?
Wieviel kostet das?
vee-FEEL KO-stet dahss?

Can I have confirmation of its receipt, please?
Kann ich eine Bestätigung des Erhaltes haben?
kahn ikh EYE-ne beh-SHTAY-tee-goong dess air-HAHL-tess HA-ben?

Over 1,000 German post offices provide a fax service called *Telebrief.*

Does this post office have Telebrief?
Hat dieses Postamt Telebrief?
haht DEE-zes POST-ahmt teh-leh-BREEF?

When will my documents arrive?
Wann werden meine Dokumente ankommen?
vahn VAIR-den MY-neh do-koo-MEN-teh AHN-ko-men?

MAIL

The main branches of German post offices are usually open from 8 a.m. to 6 p.m., Monday to Friday, and from 8 a.m. to noon on Saturdays. Mail is not delivered on Sundays, but it is collected. Smaller post offices may be closed during the 12–2 lunch hour during the week.

German postal services include registered mail, proof of delivery for registered letters, and receipts/proof of delivery for valuable goods. Express letters and packages are sent via the regular mail but are delivered by a special service between 6 a.m. and 10 p.m. (or overnight for an additional special charge). International express delivery, known as Datapost, is also available from Germany. Dialing 011605 or 11605 will yield further information about postal services.

How do I get to the post office?
Wie komme ich zu dem Postamt?
vee KO-meh ikh tsoo dem POST-ahmt?

When is it open?
Wann ist es geöffnet?
vahn isst ess geh-ERF-net?

Can I mail this from here?
Kann ich das hier versenden?
kagn ikh dahss here fair-ZEN-den?

Can you wrap this for me?
Können Sie das für mich einwickeln?
KER-nen zee dahss für mikh INE-vik-keln?

Where can I buy envelopes?
Wo kann ich Briefumschläge kaufen?
vo KAHN IKH BREEF-oom-shlay-gheh KOW-fen?

Large envelopes, please, for documents.
Große Umschläge, bitte, für Dokumente.
GRO-seh OOM-shlay-gheh, BIT-teh, für doh-koo-MEN-teh.

Where can I buy packing material?
Wo kann ich Packmaterial kaufen?
vo kahn ikh pahk-ma-teh-ree-ALL KOW-fen?

How much will it cost to mail this?
Wieviel kostet es dieses zu schicken?
vee-FEEL KO-stet ess DEE-zess tsoo SHICK-ken?

Where can I mail a letter?
Wo kann ich einen Brief abschicken?
vo kahn ikh EYE-nen breef AHB-shick-en?

I want to send a package.
Ich möchte ein Paket schicken.
ikh MERK-teh ine pa-KEHT SHICK-en.

Can you help me fill this form?
Können Sie mir helfen, dieses Formular auszufüllen?
*KERN-en zee meer HEL-fen, DEE-zess for-moo-LAR
OWSS-tsoo-FÜL-len?*

When will this arrive?
Wann wird das ankommen?
vahn veert dahss AHN-ko-men?

Is there a faster way to send this?
Gibt es eine schnelleren Weg, es zu schicken?
ghibt ess INE-nen SHNEL-ler-en vegg ess tsoo SHICK-en?

Can I send this letter Express Mail, please?
Kann ich diesen Brief per Express schicken, bitte?
kahn ikh DEE-sen breef pehr ex-PRESS SHICK-en, BIT-teh?

I'd like to send this package express.
Ich möchte das Paket gern per Eilbote schicken.
ikh MERK-teh dahss pa-KHET gairn pehr ILE-bo-teh SHICK-en.

What is the extra charge?
Wieviel kostet das extra?
vee-FEEL KO-stet dahss EX-tra?

I'd like this to arrive as soon as possible.
Ich möchte, daß es so bald wie möglich ankommt.
ikh MERK-teh dahss ess zo bahlt vee MERG-likh AHN-kohmt.

I'm willing to pay for it to be delivered at night.
Ich zahle auch für Auslieferung über Nacht.
ikh TSAHL-eh owkh für OWSS-lee-feh-roong über nakht.

I want to send this registered mail.
Ich möchte das per Einschreiben schicken.
ikh MERK-teh dahss pair INE-shry-ben SHICK-en.

Can I get a receipt when this is received?
Kann ich eine Quittung bekommen, wann es angekommen ist?
kahn ikh EYE-neh KVEE-toong beh-KO-men vahn ess
AHN-geh-ko-men isst?

How can I register these valuable goods?
Wie kann ich diese Wertsachen registrieren lassen?
vee kahn ikh DEE-zeh VAIRT-za-khen reh-ghis-TREE-ren LA-sen?

When will this package reach America?
Wann wird dieses Paket in Amerika ankommen?
vann veert dee-zess pa-KATE in ah-MEH-ree-ka ahn-KO-men?

How long will this take to get there?
Wie lange dauert dieses, bis es ankommt?
vee LAHN-geh DA-wert DEE-sess biss ess AHN-kohmt?

COURIERS

Courier service for materials, parts, or samples is available at the post office, as well as through German Federal Railways, for intra-German transport. About 50% of its stations offer same-day delivery service (*Kurierdienst*) Monday to Friday. Another type of service (*Expreßdienst*) offers same or next-morning delivery, depending on the destination. Packages weighing up to 100kg/220lb will be guaranteed arrival by 8 a.m. the following day if they are sent by 5.30 p.m. by a third type of express service (*Termindienst*). It's possible for packages to be delivered and picked up either at railway stations or door-to-door.

How do I contact the express services?
Wie kontaktiere ich den Expreßdienst?
vee kohn-tahk-TEE-reh ikh dehn ex-PRESS-deenst?

I'd like this to go by Kurierdienst, please.
Ich hätte das gern per Kurierdienst geschickt.
ikh HET-teh dahss gairn pehr koo-ree-YERR-deenst geh-SHICKT.

Can I send this by *Expreßdienst*?
Kann ich das per Expreßdienst schicken?
kahn ikh dahss pehr ex-PRESS-deenst SHICK-en?

This package is for *Termindienst*.
Dieses Päckchen ist für den Termindienst.
DEE-zess PECK-khen isst für dehn tehr-MEEN-deenst.

When will my package arrive?
Wann wird mein Paket ankommen?
vahn veert mine pa-KEHT AHN-ko-men?

How much will it cost?
Wieviel kostet es?
vee-FEEL KO-stet ess?

Is there a faster way to send this?
Gibt es einen schnelleren Weg, das zu schicken?
ghibt ess EYE-nen SHNEL-ler-en vehk dahss tsoo SHICK-en?

Is there a cheaper way to send this?
Gibt es einen billigeren Weg, das zu schicken?
ghibt ess EYE-nen BILL-eh-geh-ren vehk dahss tsoo SHICK-en?

What is your address?
Wie ist Ihre Adresse?
vee isst EE-reh ah-DREH-seh?

What is the postal code for this city?
Wie ist die Postleitzahl für diese Stadt?
vee isst dee POST-lite-tsahl für DEE-seh shtat?

SETTING UP A
BUSINESS MEETING

6

INTRODUCTIONS

Frequently, business travelers will have received an official invitation from a German organization or enterprise. In this case, the host organization will probably send officials to meet their guests at the airport – or, at the very least, will send a car and driver.

Thank you for meeting me.
Vielen Dank, daß Sie mich abgeholt haben.
FEE-len dahnk dahss zee mikh AHP-geh-holt HA-ben.

I am very happy to meet you.
Sehr erfreut, Ihre Bekanntschaft zu machen.
zair air-FROYT EE-reh beh-KAHNT-shahft tsoo MA-khen.

Thanks for sending the car.
Danke, daß Sie den Wagen geschickt haben.
DAHN-keh dahss zee dehn VA-gehn geh-SHIKT HA-ben.

I arrived at the hotel with no problems.
Ich bin in meinem Hotel ohne Probleme gut angekommen.
ikh bin in MY-nem ho-TEL o-neh pro-BLEH-meh goot
AHN-geh-ko-men.

Like many Europeans, the Germans value continuity in a business relationship. To the greatest extent possible, then, a company will benefit from continuing to send the same negotiators to Germany.

By now, we're old friends!
Jetzt sind wir bald alte Freunde.
yetzt zint veer bahlt AHL-teh FROYN-deh.

I was here last year.
Ich war letztes Jahr hier.
ikh var LET-zehs yahr here.

I had a meeting with your company last year.
Ich habe mich mit Ihrer Firma im letzten Jahr getroffen.
ikh HA-beh mikh mit EE-reh FEER-ma imm LET-zen yahr
geh-TRO-fen.

I work with (Mr. /Ms.) ——— .
Ich arbeite mit (Herrn/ Frau) ——— .
ikh ar-bite-eh mit (hairn/ frow) ——— .

Last time I spoke with (Mr./Ms.) ——— .
Das letze Mal habe ich mit (Herrn/ Frau) ——- gesprochen.
dahss LET-zeh mahl HA-beh ikh mit (hairn/ frow) ———
geh-SHPRO-khen.

I am friend of (Mr. /Ms.) ——— .
Ich bin ein Freund von (Herrn/ Frau) ——— .
ikh bin ine froynt fohn (hairn/ frow) ——— .

Germans value a level of formality that many foreigners may find exaggerated. However, it would be a mistake for foreigners to assume that this formality denotes coldness or lack of friendliness. Rather, it means that all parties can rely upon a certain way of doing things, which means that everyone can relax, secure in their mutual reliance on certain courtesies. Thus, Germans always shake hands when greeting or saying goodbye to one another.

My name is ——-.
Ich heiße ——-.
ikh HY-seh ——-.

I represent the ——- company.
Ich repräsentiere die Firma ——-.
ikh reh-preh-sen-TEE-reh dee FEER-ma ——-.

We are located in New York.
Unser Sitz ist in New York.
OON-zer sitz isst in New York.

What is your nationality?
Aus welchem Land kommen Sie?
owss VEL-khem lahnt KO-men zee?

(The principal nationalities can be found in the English–German business dictionary on pages 181–202.)

What city are you from?
Aus welcher Stadt sind Sie?
owss VEL-kher shtat zint zee?

Most of the world's large cities are spelt the same in German and English. Almost all American and British cities are spelled the same in German. Certain German cities, however, have a different form and spelling when written in English. Both German and English have their own versions of other European city names. Among the variants are: Vienna (Wien), Cologne (Köln), Munich (München), Nuremberg (Nürnberg), Florence (Florenz), Rome (Rom), and Venice (Venedig). Chemnitz, after a half-century change to Karl-Marx-Stadt, has now been changed back to Chemnitz.

The names of some countries differ from the English equivalents: Germany – **Deutschland** (*DOYTCH-lahnt*); the United States – **die Vereinigten Staaten** (*dee fair-INE-nig-ten SHTA-ten*); France – **Frankreich** (*FRAHNK-rike*); Russia – **Rußland** (*ROOS-lahnt*); Austria – **Österreich** (*ERS-tehr-rike*); Switzerland – **die Schweiz** (*dee shvyts*); Greece – **Griechenland** (*GREE-khen-lahnt*).

When will we meet again?
Wann treffen wir uns wieder?
vahn TREF-fen veer oonts VEE-der?

It was a pleasure meeting you.
Es war ein Vergnügen, Sie zu treffen.
ess var ine fairg-NÜ-ghen zee tsoo TREF-fen.

I hope to see you again soon.
Ich hoffe Sie bald wieder zu sehen.
ikh HO-feh zee bahlt VEE-der tsoo ZEY-hen.

FORMS OF ADDRESS

Forms of address are likewise quite formal in German business circles. Generally, people use full names on both business and social occasions, even when they are old acquaintances. A German would be far more likely to call an office mate "Herr Kraus" or

"Frau Schmidt" than "Josef" or "Helga." *Fräulein* is used only for young girls, not for unmarried women.

If a German has a title – which is common in German professional life – the title takes the place of the last name: "Herr Doktor," "Frau Professor," and the like. Women's titles are usually inflected to reflect a feminine ending. Germans are quite offended if their titles are not used, although they are even more offended to be addressed by titles that are not their own.

Many Germans indicate their qualifications on their business cards, letterheads, etc. Thus a person with an engineering diploma might use *Dipl. Ing.* after his or her name.

Mr.	Ms.
Herr	**Frau**
hair	*frow*
Doctor (male)	Doctor (female)
Herr Doktor	**Frau Doktor**
hair Dok-tor	*frow Dok-tor*
Professor (male)	Professor (female)
Herr Professor	**Frau Professor**
hair pro-Fess-or	*frow pro-FESS-or*
Director (male)	Director (female)
Herr Direktor	**Frau Direktor**
hair dee-REK-tor	*frow dee-REK-tor*

Some words are English adaptations:

Manager (male)   **Managerin** (female)

Foreigners should also be aware that there are two forms of address in German: the formal, using the pronoun *Sie* to mean "you"; and the informal, using the pronoun *Du*. Unless a colleague specifically suggests it, foreigners should *always* use the more formal *Sie*, regardless of what other informalities have been set up. It is quite possible for two Germans to know each other for years without ever using the *Du* form.

How are you today.
Wie geht es Ihnen heute?
vee gate ess EE-nen HOY-teh?

I'm pleased to see you again.
Ich freue mich, Sie wieder zu sehen.
ikh FROY-eh mikh zee VEE-der tsoo ZEY-hen.

I'm very pleased to be working with your company.
Es ist mir ein Vergnügen, mit Ihrer Firma zu arbeiten.
ess isst meer ine fairg-NÜ-ghen mit EE-rer FEER-ma tsoo AR-by-ten.

CONFIRMING AN APPOINTMENT

In Germany and Austria, the local company is clearly the host; hence, it is up to the German side to make arrangements for any meeting.

It goes without saying that foreigners should arrive on time for any meeting that's been arranged, since punctuality and efficiency are highly valued in Germany. Arriving even a few minutes late will create an unfavorable impression.

What are we meeting?
Wo werden wir uns treffen?
vo VAIR-den veer oonts TREF-fen?

Where is that located?
Wo liegt das?
vo leegt dahss?

Please write down the address for me.
Bitte schreiben Sie mir die Adresse auf.
BIT-teh SHRY-ben zee meere dee ah-DRESS-eh owf.

Can you tell my driver how to get there?
Können Sie meinem Fahrer sagen, wie ich dort hinkomme?
KER-nen zee mine-nem FA-rehr zahg-en, vee ikh dort HIN-ko-meh?

What day are we meeting?
An welchem Tag treffen wir uns?
ahn VEL-khem takh TREF-fen veer oonts?

What time are we meeting?
Um wieviel Uhr treffen wir uns?
oom vee-FEEL oor TREF-fen veer oonts?

How long will the meeting last?
Wie lange wird das Treffen dauern?
vee LAHN-geh veert dahss TREF-fen DOW-ern?

I'm looking forward to seeing you again.
Es wird ein Vergnügen sein, Sie wieder zu treffen.
ess veert ine fairg-NÜ-ghen zine zee VEE-der-tsoo-TREF-fen.

I'll see you at the meeting.
Ich werde Sie bei dem Treffen sehen.
ikh VAIR-deh zee by dem TREF-fen ZAY-hen.

FIRST MEETINGS
First meetings usually take place in a company office, probably in a small private conference room. Foreign travelers should not expect to meet privately with senior executives, as subordinates from key departments will probably be invited to attend. Although the meeting will be more formal than most people from English-speaking countries would be used to, a certain amount of pleasant small talk and polite questioning will take place before the meeting actually begins.

I'm enjoying your city very much.
Ich habe sehr viel Spaß in Ihrer Stadt.
ikh HA-beh zair feel shpahss in EE-reh shtaht.

Have you lived here long?
Wohnen Sie hier schon lange?
VO-nen zee here shown LAHN-geh?

I was born in ___, but now I live in ___.
Ich bin in ___ geboren, wohne jetzt aber in ___.
ikh bin in ___ geh-BO-ren, VO-neh yetzt AH-bair in ___.

Were you ever in America?
Waren Sie jemals in Amerika?
VA-ren zee YAY-mahlz in ah-MEH-ree-ka?

My trip was very pleasant.
Meine Reise war sehr angenehm.
MINE-eh RYE-seh var sair AHN-geh-nehm.

I had no trouble finding your office.
Ich hatte keine Schwierigkeiten, Ihr Büro zu finden.
ikh HA-teh KYE-neh SHVEE-rig-kye-ten ear bü-RO tsoo FIN-den.

Your directions were excellent!
Ihre Wegbeschreibung war hervorragend!
EE-reh VEHG-beh-shry-boong var hair-VOR-rah-gent!

BUSINESS TITLES

Committed as they are to hierarchies, German businesspeople will be interested to know the ranks of those with whom they are dealing. Foreign negotiators may be asked detailed questions about their staffs, as well as about other aspects of their operations.

I am the president.
Ich bin der Präsident.
ikh bin dehr preh-zee-DENT.

I am the vice-president.
Ich bin der Vize-Präsident.
ikh bin dehr VEE-tseh preh-zee-DENT.

I am the manager.
Ich bin der Geschäftsführer.
ikh bin dehr geh-SHAYFTS-fü-rehr.

I am a senior official.
Ich bin ein leitender Beamter.
ikh bin ine LY-ten-dehr beh-AHM-tehr.

He is an engineer.
Er ist Ingenieur.
er ist en-zhen-YEUR.

She is an engineer.
Sie ist Ingenieurin.
zee isst en-zhen-YEUR-in.

He is a lawyer.
Er ist Rechtsanwalt.
air isst REKTS-ahn-vault.

She is a lawyer.
Sie ist Rechtsanwältin.
zee isst REKTS-ahn-velt-in.

This is my superior, Mr. /Ms. ___ .
Das ist mein Vorgesetzer, Herr/Frau ___ .
Das isst mine for-geh-ZETZ-er, hair/frow ___ .

My superior will be at the signing tomorrow.
Mein Vorgesetzter wird morgen bei der Unterzeichnung anwesend sein.
Mine for-geh-ZETZ-ter veert MOR-ghen by dehr oon-ter-ZYKE-noong an-weh-zent zine.

SUBMITTING A PROPOSAL

Although German businesspeople may interrogate their foreign counterparts as a way of gaining information, they will also diligently peruse any written matter submitted to them. Foreign business people will almost certainly find it useful to come equipped with a written proposal, preferably translated into German.

Have you seen our proposal?
Haben Sie sich unseren Vorschlag angesehen?
HA-ben zee zikh OON-sern FOR-shlahg AHN-geh-zay-hen?

We sent you a proposal last month.
Wir haben Ihnen letzten Monat einen Vorschlag zugeschickt.
veer HA-ben EE-nen LET-zen MO-naht INE-en FOR-shlahg tsoo-geh-SHIKT.

Here is our latest proposal.
Hier ist unser neuester Vorschlag.
here isst OON-ser NOY-ess-tehr FOR-shlahg.

What do you think of our proposal?
Was halten Sie von unserem Vorschlag?
vahss HAHL-ten zee fohn OON-seh-rem FOR-shlahg?

Would you like to see a written proposal?
Würden Sie gerne einen schriftlichen Vorschlag sehen?
VUR-den zee GAIR-neh EYE-nen SHRIFT-lee-khen FOR-shlahg ZAY-en?

What other information do you need?
Welche anderen Information brauchen Sie?
VEL-kheh AHN-deh-rehn in-for-mahts-YOHN BROW-khen zee?

Do you have any questions?
Haben Sie irgendwelche Fragen?
HA-ben zee EER-gend-VEL-khe FRA-ghen?

(Mr. /Ms.) —— can answer that question for you.
Herr/Frau —— wird Ihnen diese Frage beantworten.
hair/frow —— veert EE-nen DEE-seh FRA-geh beh-AHNT-vor-ten.

(Mr./Ms.) —— will call you about that.
Herr/Frau —— wird Sie darüber anrufen.
hair/frow —— veert see da-RÜ-ber AHN-roo-fen.

(Mr./Ms.) —— will send you that information.
Herr/Frau —— wird Ihnen diese Information schicken.
hair/frow —— veert EE-nen DEE-seh in-for-mahts-YOHN SHIK-ken.

I don't know, but I'll find out.
Das weiß ich nicht, aber ich werde es herausfinden.
dahss vice ikh nikht, AH-ber ikh VAIR-deh ess hair-OWSS-fin-den.

I'll ask our engineering department.
Ich werde unsere Konstruktions-Abteilung fragen.
ikh VAIR-deh OON-zeh-reh kohnt-strook-ts' yohns AHB-tile-oong FRA-ghen.

I'll ask our legal department.
Ich werde unsere Rechtsabteilung fragen.
ikh VAIR-deh OON-zeh-reh rekhts-AHB-tile-oong FRA-ghen.

I'll ask my superior.
Ich werde meinen Vorgesetzten fragen.
ikh VAIR-deh MY-nen FOR-geh-zets-ten FRA-ghen.

I'll ask our company president.
Ich werde unseren Firmenpräsidenten fragen.
ikh VAIR-deh OON-zeh-ren FEER-men-preh-zee-DEN-ten FRA-ghen.

INTERPRETERS

Foreign travelers should not assume that all or even most German negotiators will speak English. When the meeting is first arranged, the German host will most likely provide an interpreter, if necessary, but the foreign businessman might want to confirm that such arrangements have in fact been made.

I am sorry, we don't speak German very well.
Es tut mir leid, wir sprechen nicht so gut deutsch.
ess toot meer lite, veer spreh-khen nihkt zo goot doytsch.

Can you bring an interpreter?
Können Sie einen Dolmetscher mitbringen?
KERN-nen zee EYE-nen DOHL-met-sher MITT-bring-en?

Or would you like us to bring an interpreter?
Oder möchten Sie, daß wir einen Dolmetscher mitbringen?
OH-dehr MERHK-ten zee dahss veer EYE-nen DOHL-met-sher MITT-bring-en?

Our colleague speaks German
Unser Kollege spricht deutsch
OON-zer ko-LAY-geh shprikht doytch

and can serve as an interpreter.
und kann als Dolmetscher dienen.
oont kahn ahlz DOHL-met-sher DEE-nen.

Thank you for the interpreter.
Wir danken Ihren für den Dolmetscher.
veer DAHNKEN EE-nen für dehn DOHL-met-sher.

TOWARD AN AGREEMENT

Coming to agreement about a contract is likely to take more than one meeting – possibly even more than one visit. The Germans are polite and efficient negotiators, but they must negotiate a network of departments and administrative levels in the course of reaching a decision. They may not acknowledge the considerable expenditure of time, money, and personnel represented by the foreign company's simple presence in Germany.

I have to return home soon.
Ich muß bald zurück nach Hause.
ikh moose bahlt tsoo-RÜK nahkh HOW-zeh.

I must fly home tomorrow.
Ich muß morgen nach Hause fliegen.
ikh mooss MOR-ghen nahkh HOW-zeh FLEE-ghen.

I must go home next week.
Ich muß nächste Woche nach Hause gehen.
ikh moose NEX-teh VO-kheh nahkh HOW-zeh GEH-en.

When can you decide?
Wann können Sie sich entschließen?
vahn KER-nen zee zikh ent-SHLEE-sen?

SETTING UP A BUSINESS MEETING

When will ___ be available?
Wann wird ___ zur Verfügung stehen?
vahn veert ___ tsoor fair-FÜ-goong shteh-en?

Will it be possible to have an answer soon?
Wäre es möglich Ihre Antwort bald zu erhalten?
*VEH-reh ess MERG-lihkh EE-reh ANT-vort bahlt tsoo
air-HAHLT-en?*

We must meet again as soon as possible.
Wir müßen uns so bald wie möglich wiedertreffen.
veer MÜ-ssen oonts zo bahlt vee merk-likh VEE-dehr-treffen.

Thank you for meeting with us.
Wir danken Ihnen für das Treffen.
veer DAHN-ken EE-nen für dahss TREF-fen.

CONDUCTING A
BUSINESS MEETING

7

THE PRELIMINARIES

As we have seen, the meeting is likely to be in a room arranged for by the German negotiator, probably a special conference room.

Every series of negotiations should begin with general introductions and hand-shaking all round. Almost invariably, a foreign business visitor will meet with at least two German negotiators at a time. That way, the superior has the support of key people from relevant departments.

Please introduce me to your colleague.
Bitte stellen Sie mich ihrem Kollegen vor.
BIT-teh SHTEH-len zee mikh EE-rem ko-LEG-en for.

I am happy to meet all of you.
Ich freue mich, Sie alle kennenzulernen.
ikh FROY-eh mikh zee AH-leh KEN-nen-tsoo-LEHR-nen.

Foreigners may wish to exchange business cards at the introductory meeting. They should make sure to carry enough cards to supply all members of the German team.

Greetings!
Gruße!
GRŮ-seh!

We are happy to meet you.
Es freut uns, Sie kennenzulernen
ess froyt oons zehr, zee KEN-nen tsoo LEHR-nen.

Thank you for inviting us to this meeting.
Vielen Dank für ihre Einladung.
FEE-len dahnk für EE-reh INE-la-doong.

We are very glad to see you here.
Es freut uns sehr, Sie zu sehen.
ess froyt oons zehr zee tsoo ZEH-en.

My name is ____ and I am the ( ) of my Company.
Ich heiße ____ und ich bin ( ) meiner Firma.

ikh HY-seh ____ oont ikh bin (   ) MY-ner FEER-ma.

This is the President of our company.
Das ist der Präsident unserer Firma.
dahss isst dehr preh-zee-DENT OON-zeh-rer FEER-ma.

Here is my card.
Hier ist meine Karte.
here isst MY-neh KAR-teh.

May I ask for your card?
Darf ich um Ihre Karte bitten?
darf ikh oom EE-reh KAR-teh BIT-ten?

In addition to business cards, it's a good idea for foreign visitors to have a brief profile of their company, translated into German. This profile can be presented to the other side after the initial exchange of business cards.

Here is some information about our company.
Hier sind einige Informationen über unsere Firma.
Here zint EYE-nee-geh in-for-maht-S'YOHN-en EW-ber OON-sehreh FEER-ma.

This includes our records for the past year.
Das enthält unsere Akten (Unterlagen) vom vergangenen Jahr.
dahss ent-HELT OON-zeh-reh AHK-ten (OON-ter-lah-ghen) fohm fair-GAHNG-en-en yar.

SMALL TALK
Meetings usually begin with small talk, despite the limited time that may be available. Appropriate topics include the weather, holidays, non-controversial current events, and remarks about one's own country.

It's a lovely day isn't it?
Es ist ein schöner Tag, nicht wahr?
ess isst ine SHER-nehr tahk, nikht var?

Is it always so cold this time of year?
Ist es immer so kalt zu dieser Jahreszeit?
isst ess IM-mehr zo kahlt tsoo DEE-zer YA-res-tsite?

Do you think it will rain?
Denken Sie, daß es regnen wird?
DEN-ken zee dahss ess REHG-nen veert?

Is it likely to snow?
Ist es möglich, daß es schneien wird?
isst ess MERG-lickh dahss ess SCHNY-en veert?

I'm looking forward to Christmas.
Ich freue mich auf Weihnachten.
ikh FROY-eh mikh owf VY-nahkh-ten.

This is a very impressive trade fair.
Das ist eine sehr beeindruckende Messe.
dahss isst EYE-neh zehr beh-ine-DROO-cken-deh MES-seh.

Did you have a pleasant weekend?
Hatten Sie ein schönes Wochenende?
Hat-en zee ine SHERN-es VO-khen-en-deh?

I'm enjoying my stay in your city very much.
Ich genieße meinen Aufenthalt in ihrer Stadt.
ikh geh-NEE-zeh mine-nen OWF-ent-hahlt in EAR-ehr shtat.

TAKING A BREAK
The German workday usually begins at 9 a.m., although in some cases appointments may be scheduled for 8.30 a.m. or even 8 a.m. The day is over by 5 p.m., although many managers stay from 5 p.m. to 7 p.m. to take advantage of the uninterrupted work time – and the time to reach New Yorkers when it's morning in New York!

Lunch is usually taken early, at noon or so, and usually lasts only an hour or so – an hour and a half in special circumstances. Company canteens usually provide good food, and foreigners may well be taken to lunch there. Negotiations are almost never scheduled during evenings and weekends – a time during which foreigners often profit by studying the documents produced at the meeting of the day.

Is it time for lunch?
Ist es Zeit zum Mittagessen?
isst ess tsite tsoom mit-tahk-ES-sen?

When will we break for lunch?
Wann haben wir Mittagspause?
vahn HA-ben veer MIT-tahks-POW-zeh?

Can we continue this discussion after lunch?
Können wir diese Unterhaltung nach dem Mittagessen fort-setzen?
KERN-nen veer DEE-seh OON-tehr-HAL-toong nahkh dehm MIT-tahk-ES-sen FORT-zet-sen?

Is this your company's canteen?
Ist das die Kantine Ihrer Firma?
isst dahss dee kahn-TEE-neh EE-rer FEER-ma?

You have very good facilities.
Sie sind gut eingerichtet.
zee zint goot INE-geh-rikh-tet.

This is a delicious lunch.
Das Mittagessen ist sehr schmackhaft!
dahss MIT-tahk-ES-sen isst zehr SHMAHK-haft!

When do we meet tomorrow?
Wann treffen wir uns morgen?
vahn TREF-fen veer oons MOR-ghen?

I'm looking forward to our next conversation.
Ich freue mich auf unser nächstes Gespräch.
ikh FROY-eh mikh owf OON-zer NEX-tes geh-SPREKH.

THE NEGOTIATIONS

As already mentioned, German negotiators will respond best to firm politeness and will respond worst to aggression or hostility. Foreign negotiators who appear inflexible may provoke an end to the negotiations; therefore it's important to avoid saying "no" even to apparently outrageous demands. Instead, negotiators should seek to appear willing to at least consider every proposal.

I'm sure we can come to an agreement.
Ich bin überzeugt, daß wir zu einer Übereinstimmung kommen werden.
*ikh bin ů-behr-tsoygt dahss veer tsoo EYE-ner
ů-behr-INE-shtim-moong ko-men VEHR-den.*

I think we need to talk further.
Ich glaube, daß wir uns noch weiter darüber unterhalten müssen.
*ikh GLAU-be, dahss veer oons nohkh VY-ter DAH-rů-ber
oon-ter-HAHL-ten můs-sen.*

Where do you disagree?
Wo stimmen Sie nicht überein?
Vo shtim-men zee nihkt ů-beh-rine?

Which points don't you accept?
Welche Punkte akzeptieren Sie nicht?
VEL-keh POONK-teh akt-zep-TEE-ren zee nihkt?

Can you explain it to me more?
Können Sie mir das noch einmal erklären?
KERN-nen zee meer dahss nohkh INE-mal air-KLEH-ren?

Let me be sure I understand you.
Lassen Sie mich gewiß sein, daß ich Sie verstehe.
LA-sen zee mikh geh-VISS zine, dahss ikh zee fair-SHTAY-eh.

This meeting will produce good things for both of us.
Dieses Treffen wird für uns Beide von Nutzen sein.
dee-SESS TREF-fen veert fůr oonts BY-deh fohn NUT-sen zine.

I have a problem with Clause Number six.
Ich habe ein Problem mit Klausel Nummer sechs.
ikh HA-beh ine pro-BLEHM mitt KLOW-zehl NOO-mehr sex.

I don't understand this point.
Ich verstehe nicht diesen Punkt.
ikh fair-SHTAY-heh nikht DEE-zen poonkt.

German negotiators will expect their foreign counterparts to talk in very specific terms. They may well ask for a great deal of detailed information. Visitors who can't readily answer detailed technical questions will become objects of either suspicion or lack of respect.

What else would you like to know?
Was möchten Sie noch wissen?
vahss MERK-ten zee nohkh VISS-en?

Could you please repeat your question?
Können Sie bitte Ihre Frage wiederholen?
KERN-nen zee BIT-teh EE-reh FRA-gheh VEE-dehr-ho-len?

Perhaps I haven't explained clearly.
Vielleicht war ich nicht klar.
feel-LYE'KT var ikh nihkt klar.

I can get that information for you in writing.
Ich kann diese Information für Sie schriftlich besorgen.
ikh kahn DEE-zeh een-for-mahts-YOHN für zee SHRIFT-likh be-zorg-en.

I will call our home office and have that information for you tomorrow.
Ich werde unser Zentral-Büro anrufen und die Informationen morgen für Sie haben.
ikh VAIR-deh OON-zer tsent-RAHL-bü-ro AHN-roo-fen oont dee een-for-mahts-YOHN-en MOR-ghen für zee HA-ben.

Mr. (Ms.) —- has that information.
Herr (Frau) —- hat diese Informationen.
hair (frow) — haht DEE-zeh een-for-mahts-YOHN-en.

GETTING AROUND WITHIN A CITY

8

TAXIS

The business traveler in Germany is mostly likely to travel by taxi. As we have said, taxis are usually not available through hailing on the street, but must either be found at a taxi rank or ordered by telephone. Hotel personnel may be useful in finding a taxi.

Can you call a taxi for me, please?
Können Sie mir bitte eine Taxi rufen?
KERN-nen zee meer BIT-teh EYE-neh TAHK-see ROO-fen?

Take me to this address please.
Fahren Sie mich zu dieser Adresse, bitte.
FA-ren zee mikh tsoo DEE-zer ah-DRES-seh BIT-teh.

Driver, how long does the trip take?
Fahrer, wie lange dauert die Fahrt?
FA-rer, vee LAHN-geh DOW-ert dee fahrt?

Do you have change?
Haben Sie Wechselgeld?
HA-ben zee VEK-zel-ghelt?

What does the trip cost?
Was kostet die Fahrt?
vahss KO-stet dee fahrt?

For other information and phrases relating to taxis, see pages 53–55. However, other means of transportation are available in most German cities.

CAR RENTAL

It is generally possible to rent a car, with or without a driver. To find a local driver, travelers might make arrangements with their travel agencies ahead of time, ask at their hotels, or inquire at local tourist offices.

I'd like to rent a car with a driver, please.
Ich möchte gern einen Wagen mit Fahrer mieten.
ikh MERK-teh gairn EYE-nen VA-ghen mitt FA-rer MEE-ten.

GETTING AROUND WITHIN A CITY

I've already reserved a car and driver.
Ich habe schon einen Wagen mit Fahrer reserviert.
ikh HA-beh shohn EYE-nen VA-ghen mitt FA-rer re-zair-VEERT.

I made the arrangements through ___ .
Ich habe eine Bestellung durch ___ gemacht.
ikh HA-beh EYE-neh beh-SHTEL-loong doorkh ___ geh-MAHKT.

How soon will a car and driver be available?
Wann wäre ein Wagen mit Fahrer zu haben?
vahn VEH-reh ine VAH-gen mitt FA-rer tsoo HA-ben?

Are there other car-rental offices near here?
Gibt es andere Autovermietungen in der Nähe?
geebt ess AHN-deh-reh OW-toh-fair-MEE-tungen in dehr NEH-heh?

How much does it cost to rent a car with driver?
Was kostet es einen Wagen mit Fahrer zu mieten?
Vahss KO-stet ess EYE-nen VAH-gen mitt FA-rer tsoo MEE-ten?

Travelers with a valid national or international driving license may drive in Germany for up to one year (after which time they must apply for a German license). Third-party insurance is compulsory for car rental.

German regulations require seat belts to be worn at all times by both front- and back-seat passengers.

The following organizations are available for car rental in Germany (for telephone numbers, please see "Addresses"):

Hertz	– offices in main cities and at all airports
Avis	– offices in main cities and at all airports
Budget	– Known as Sixt in Germany; offices in all large towns; at main airports
Europcar	– has about 80 outlets in Germany
Interrent	– has about 40 railway station outlets and at main airports

I would like to rent a car, please.
Ich möchte gern ein Auto mieten.
ikh MERK-teh gairn ine OW-toh MEE-ten.

Give me the daily rate.
Was kostet das am Tag?
vahs KO-stet dahss ahm tahk?

I would like to rent by the half-day.
Ich möchte das gern für einen halben Tag mieten.
ikh MERK-teh dahss gairn für INE-nen HAHL-ben tahk MEE-ten.

by the hour.
pro Stunde.
proh SHTOON-deh.

Do you have a street map?
Haben Sie einen Stadtplan?
HA-ben zee EYE-nen STAHT-plahn?

How do I get to ___?
Wie komme ich zu ___?
vee KO-meh ikh tsoo ___?

Here is my driver's license.
Hier ist mein Führerschein.
here isst mine FÜ-rer-shine.

Where do I buy insurance?
Wo bekomme ich Versicherung?
vo beh-KO-meh ikh fair-ZIK-hair-roong?

How do the seatbelts work?
Wie funktionieren die Sicherheitsgurte?
vee foonk-ts-yohn-EE-ren dee ZIK-kher-hites-gur-teh?

German regulations on drinking and driving are quite strict: the equivalent of no more than a half-liter or pint of beer. There is no general speed limit on the highway (*Autobahn*), although watch out for sections with limits. The police will stop a car that is too close to the one in front. Most roads have a maximum limit of 100 kmph/62mph; in built-up areas, the limit goes down to 50 kmph/31mph.

I'm sorry, officer; I am a tourist here.
Ich bedauere es sehr, Herr Wachtmeister, ich bin Tourist hier.
Ikh beh-DOW-eh-reh ess zehr, hair VAKH-my-ster, ikh bin
TOO-rist here.

PUBLIC TRANSPORT

Public transportation in Germany is clean, efficient, and relatively easy for the foreign traveler to understand. Railways, buses, street-cars, and subways (if any) are all integrated in the major cities, so that local travel is convenient.

Tickets can be purchased at kiosks or vending machines either individually or in strips of 10 or 12 known as a *Mehrfahrtenkarte* or a *Streifenkarte*. These multi-ride tickets cost around DM 15. Individual tickets must be canceled before boarding or while on the vehicle. The cancelers (*Entwerter*), are near the entrances.

A traveler may also buy a one-day tourist ticket, which costs from DM 6 to DM 10. The day tickets allow full use of public transportation during a 24-hour period.

Where can I buy a bus ticket?
Wo kann ich eine Busfahrkarte kaufen?
vo kahn ikh EYE-neh BOOS-far-kar-teh KOW-fen?

... a streetcar ticket?
... Straßenbahnfahrkarte kaufen?
... STRA-sen-bahn-far-kar-teh KOW-fen?

I'd like to buy a multi-ride ticket, please.
Ich möchte bitte eine Sammelkarte kaufen.
· *ikh MERK-teh BIT-teh EYE-neh ZAM-mel-kar-teh KOW-fen.*

How much is it?
Wie teuer ist sie?
vee TOY-er isst zee?

How many rides is it good for?
Für wieviele Fahrten ist diese?
für vee-FEE-leh FAHR-ten isst DEE-zeh?

I want a ticket to the Kurfürstendamm.
Ich möchte eine Karte zum Kurfürstendamm.
ikh MERK-teh EYE-neh KAR-teh tsoom koor-FÜRS-ten-dam.

Where do I cancel this ticket?
Wo kann ich diesen Fahrshein entwerten?
vo kahn ikh DEE-zen FAHR-shine ent-VAIR-ten?

I'm going to _____ .
Ich fahre nach _____ .
ikh FA-reh nach _____ .

Can you tell me where to get off?
Können Sie mir sagen, wo ich aussteigen muß?
KERN-en zee meer SA-ghen vo ikh OWS-sty-ghen moose?

Those German cities that have a suburban railway (*S-Bahn*) or an underground railway (*U-Bahn*) are justly proud of their quiet, clean, and efficient working. Businesspeople often take above ground or underground trains to the appropriate stop and than find a taxi for the last leg of the journey, rather than switching to a tram or bus. During major trade fairs, however, everyone travels by tram. Bus routes are more complicated than other forms of public transport, but trade fairs may offer special buses to and from the airport or railway station.

Where is the nearest subway station?
Wo ist die nächste U-Bahnstation?
vo isst die NEX-teh OO-bahn-sta-ts'yohn?

Where is the nearest train station?
Wo ist der nächste Bahnhof?
vo isst dehr NEX-teh BAHN-hof?

I want to go to the Opera House.
Ich will zum Opernhaus.
ikh vill tsoom O-pern-House.

Which stop is that?
Welche Haltestelle ist das?
VEL-kheh HAHLT-eh-stell-eh isst dahss?

How many stops to the Olympia Stadium?
Wieviele Haltestellen sind es zum Olympia-Stadium?
*vee FEE-leh HAHLT-eh-stell-en zint ess tsoom
O-LYMP-ya-STA-dee-yoom?*

Where is the map?
Wo ist die Linienkarte?
vo isst dee LEEN-yen-KAR-teh?

Where can I get change?
Wo kann ich Kleingeld bekommen?
vo kahn ikh KLINE-gelt beh-KO-men?

ON FOOT

By the way, in good weather, it's a pleasure to walk through most
German cities. Sidewalks are wide and well-maintained, and cafés
and shops offer interesting prospects to the traveler who is not in
too much of a hurry. Foreigners will find German citizens extremely
helpful and hospitable, many of them speak passable English.

Excuse me, I want to go to ——.
Verzeihung, ich möchte zu ——.
fair-TSY-hoong, ikh merkhte tsoo ——.

Where is that on the map?
Wo kann ich das auf der Karte finden?
vo kahn ikh dahss owf dair KAR-teh FIN-den?

Thank you for your help!
Danke für Ihre Hilfsbereitschaft!
DAHN-keh für EE-reh HEELFS-beh-RITE-shaft!

TRAVEL BETWEEN CITIES

9

German travelers themselves tend to drive on most journeys under 200km (125 miles) or so. For longer trips, say, up to 500km (300 miles), a German traveler will take a train. Planes are used to make journeys that are longer still – or if there is a convenient commuter flight.

BY AIR
Frankfurt am Main is the air hub of Germany, serving as the head-quarters for Lufthansa.

To the airport, please.
Zum Flugplatz, bitte.
tsoom FLOOG-plahtz BIT-teh.

How long does it take to go to the airport?
Wie lange dauert es zum Flughafen?
vee LAHN-geh DOW-ert ess tsoom FLOOG-ha-fen?

How long does the flight to ___ take?
Wie lange dauert der Flug nach ___?
vee LAHN-geh DOW-ert dehr floog nahkh ___?

I want a ticket to ___ please.
Ich hätte gern einen Flugschein nach ___ .
ikh HEH-teh gairn EYE-nen FLOOG-shine nahkh ___ .

What time does the flight leave?
Um wieviel Uhr geht der Flug?
oom VEE-feel oor gayt dehr floog?

When does the flight arrive?
Wann kommt der Flug an?
vahn kohmt dehr floog ahn?

Making and Changing Reservations
Reservations for air travel should be made about two days in advance. Tickets will most likely be booked through Lufthansa, though of course other airlines serve Germany as well. Hotel service bureau or local travel agencies may be of assistance. (For Lufthansa's direct numbers, see "Addresses.")

I've already made these reservations.
Ich habe diese Reservierungen schon gemacht.
ikh HA-beh DEE-zeh reh-ser-vee-ROON-ghen shown geh-MAHKT.

I'd like to confirm my reservation.
Ich möchte meine Reservierung bestätigen.
ikh MERK-teh MY-neh reh-ser VEE-roong beh-SHTAY-tee-ghen.

Where can I make reservations?
Wo kann ich Reservierungen machen?
vo kahn ikh reh-ser-vee-ROON-ghen MA-khen?

Can you arrange for a driver to meet me, please?
Können Sie mir bitte einen Fahrer besorgen, der mich abholt?
KER-nen zee meer BIT-teh EYE-nen FA-rer beh-ZOR-ghen, dehr mikh AP-holt?

Can you reserve a rental car for me as well?
Können Sie mir auch ein Auto mieten?
KERN-en zee meer owkh ine ow-toh MEE-ten?

I'd like to change my reservation.
Ich möchte meine Reservierung verändern.
ikh MERK-teh MY-neh reh-ser-VEE-roong ver-EN-dern.

I'd like to cancel my reservation.
Ich möchte meine Reservierung stornieren.
ikh MERK-eh MY-neh reh-ser-VEE-roong shtohr-NEE-ren.

How much will it cost to cancel?
Was kostet eine Stornierung?
vahss KO-stet EYE-neh shtohr-NEE-roong?

Lufthansa offers few discounts on fares. Sometimes, when travelers have an international ticket, it can be combined with a domestic flight for a 40% reduction, but there may be so many restrictions on that arrangement as to limit its usefulness for a business traveler. First-class fares are 50% higher than economy. Surprisingly, they are available only through Lufthansa and Swissair.

I want a first-class ticket, please.
Ich hätte gern einen Flugschein erster Klasse, bitte.
ikh heh-teh gairn EYE-nen FLOOG-shine AIR-steh KLA-seh
BIT-teh.

Please give me business class.
Bitte geben Sie mir Geschäftsklasse.
BIT-teh GAY-ben zee meer geh-SHEFTS-kla-seh.

I would like tourist class, please.
Ich möchte Touristenklasse bitte.
ikh MERK-teh too-RISS-ten-kla-seh BIT-teh.

This ticket has the wrong time.
Dieser Flugsschein hat die falsche Zeit.
DEE-se FLOOG-shine haht dee FAHL-sheh tsite.

The wrong amount has been deducted here.
Hier ist der falsche Betrag abgezogen worden.
here isst dehr FAHL-sheh be-TRAHG AHB-geh-tsoh-gen VOR-den.

How can I qualify for the lower fare?
Wie bekomme ich einen niedrigeren Tarif?
vee beh-KO-meh ikh EYE-nen NEED-ree-geh-ren ta-REEF?

Travel Times

Lufthansa is one of the most efficient airlines in the world, with an admirable on-time record. However, it is least likely to maintain this record during peak travel times, when the increase in domestic traffic has placed an enormous strain on air travel facilities.

From which gate does my flight leave?
Von welchem Ausgang geht mein Flug ab?
fohn VEL-khem OWSS-gahng gayt mine floog ahb?

Excuse me, where is gate ___?
Verzeihung, wo ist Ausgang Nummer ___?
fair-TSY-oong, vo isst OWSS-gahng NOOM-mer ___?

Where do I check in for this flight?
Wo melde ich mich für den Flug an?
vo MEL-deh ikh mikh für den floog ahn?

Where do I check my baggage?
Wo gebe ich mein Gepäck auf?
vo GAY-beh ikh mine geh-PECK owf?

Can I take this on the plane with me?
Kann ich das mit auf das Flugzeug nehmen?
kahn ikh dass mit owf dahss FLOOG-tsoig NEH-men?

Has flight number ___ been delayed?
Ist Flug Nummer ___ verspätet?
isst floog NOOM-mer ___ fair-SPAY-tet?

When will my flight leave?
Wann wird mein Flug abfliegen?
vahn veert mine floog AHB-flee-ghen?

Is this flight on time?
Ist dieser Flug pünktlich?
isst DEE-zer floog pünkt-lickh?

How long is the delay?
Wie lange ist die Verspätung?
vee LAHN-geh isst dee fair SPAY-toong?

When is the new departure time?
Wie ist die neue Abflugszeit?
vee isst dee NOY-eh AHB-floogs-tsite?

When is the new arrival time?
Was ist die neue Ankunftszeit?
vas isst dee NOY-eh AHN-koonfts-tsite?

Will there be an announcement?
Wird der Flug angesagt?
veert dehr floog AHN-ge-zahkt?

Will the announcement be in English, also?
Wird die Ansage auch in englisch erfolgen?
veert dee AHN-za-geh owkh in EHNG-lish ehr-FOL-gen?

How long should I wait?
Wie lange soll ich warten?
vee LAHN-geh zoll ikh VAR-ten?

When will you have more information?
Wann werden Sie mehr Informationen haben?
vann VAIR-den zee mare in-for-mahts-YOHN-en HA-ben?

Refreshments and Facilities
There is often no in-flight food or beverage service on Lufthansa
for internal flights but snacks may be sold at the departure gate.

Is any food served on this flight?
Servieren Sie Speisen auf diesem Flug?
sair-VEE-ren zee SHPY-zen owf DEE-zem floog?

Do you serve drinks on this flight?
Servieren Sie Getränke auf diesem Flug?
sair-VEE-ren zee geh-TRENK-eh owf DEE-zem floog?

Is there a restaurant in this airport?
Gibt es ein Restaurant auf diesem Flughafen?
gibt ess ine res-tau-RAHNT owf DEE-zem FLOOG-ha-fen?

Is there a gift shop in the airport?
Gibt es einen Geschenkladen im Flughafen?
gibt ess EYE-nen geh-SHENK-la-den imm FLOOG-ha-fen?

Where are the toilets?
Wo sind die Toiletten?
vo sint dee twa-LET-ten?

Excuse me, may I have something to drink?
Verzeihung, darf ich etwas zu trinken haben?
FER-tsy-oong, darf ikh ET-vahs tsoo TRINK-en HA-ben?

... something to eat?
... etwas zu essen haben?
... ET-vahs tsoo ES-sen HA-ben?

On Disembarking
Once at the airport, personnel are usually courteous and helpful. Although many will likely speak English, they may appreciate a traveler's effort to converse in German.

Where do I pick up my bags?
Wo hole ich mein Gepäck ab?
vo HO-leh ikh mine geh-PECK ahb?

How do I get to the —- Hotel?
Wie komme ich zum Hotel —-?
vee KO-meh ikh tsoom ho-TEL —?

A car will pick me up.
Ein Auto wird mich abholen.
ine OW-toh veert mikh AHB-ho-len.

Where does it stop?
Wo wird es halten?
vo VEERT ess HAHL-ten?

I've arranged to rent a car.
Ich habe ein Auto gemietet.
ikh HA-beh ine OW-toh geh-MEE-tet.

Where do I pick it up?
Wo hole ich es ab?
vo HO-leh ikh es ahb?

BY RAIL
German Trains
Traveling by train is one of the pleasures of a trip to Europe, and in Germany, most travelers will enjoy time spent on the German Federal Railways (*Deutsche Bundesbahn* or DB). Trains in Germany are rated by speed and by the importance of the route.

Here are the major categories, in descending order of importance:

EC or Eurocity trains –	These travel the length of the country.
IC or Intercity trains –	These run between main cities at regular hourly times, and are the preferred means of travel for business travelers. They are equipped with telephones on which calls can be both made and received, at twice the rate of a pay phone. Their speed ranges from 100 kmph/60mph to 130 kmph/80mph.
FD or long-distance expresses –	These fast trains travel outside the intercity network.
D-Zug –	Other fast trains run with less regularity than the IC lines.
E-Zug –	These trains also run outside the IC system, and are less fast than the D-Züge.
S-Bahn –	Urban/surburban trains running in Hamburg, the Ruhr, Frankfurt, Stüttgart, and Munich; they're integrated with local public transport.

To the railroad station, please.
Zum Bahnhof, bitte.
Tsoom BAHN-hohf, BIT-teh.

I want a ticket to ____ .
Ich möchte eine Fahrkarte nach ____ .
ikh MERK-teh INE-neh FAR-kar-teh nahkh ____ .

Travel Times
Here are some of the average travel times for IC trains:
  Hanover–Düsseldorf – 2 hours, 20 minutes
  Frankfurt–Bonn – 2 hours
  Munich–Nuremberg – 1 hour, 40 minutes
  Mannheim–Stüttgart – 1 hour, 30 minutes

How long is the trip to ___?
Wie lange dauert die Fahrt nach ___?
vee LAHN-geh DOW-wert dee fahrt nahkh ___?

When does this train reach ___?
Wann kommt dieser Zug in ___ an?
vahn kohmt DEE-zer tsoog in ___ ahn?

When does the train leave?
Wann fährt der Zug ab?
vahn fairt dehr tsoog ahb?

When does the next train leave for ___?
Wann fährt der nächste Zug nach ___ ab?
vahn fairt dehr NEX-teh tsoog nakh ___ ahb?

Is there an earlier train to ___?
Gibt es einen früheren Zug nach ___?
ghibt ess INE-en FRUH-heh-ren tsoog nahkh ___?

Is there a later train to ___?
Gibt es einen späteren Zug nach ___?
ghibt ess EYE-nen SH' PAY-teh-ren tsoog nahkh ___?

Making and Changing Reservations

Although it is certainly possible to buy train tickets on the spot, reservations are advised for the business traveler on a tight schedule, particularly for those traveling during peak hours. Travel agencies will reserve seats for all or part of a journey. The traveler will find the reserved seat is marked by a card giving all details.

Can I still make reservations for this date?
Kann ich noch Reservierungen für dieses Datum machen?
kahn ikh nohkh reh-zair-VEE-roon-gen für DEE-zess DA-toom MA-khen?

I want to change my reservation on this train.
Ich möchte meine Reservierung auf diesen Zug ändern.
ikh MERK-teh MY-neh reh-zair-VEE-roong owf DEE-zen tsoog END-ern.

I want to cancel my reservation on this train.
Ich möchte meine Reservierung auf diesem Zug stornieren.
*ikh MERK-teh MY-neh reh-zair-VEE-roong owf DEE-sem tsoog
shtohr-nee-ren.*

Where is seat number ___?
Wo ist Sitz Nummer ___?
vo isst ZITZ-NOO-mer ___?

On the Train

Major train stations feature a diagram of each train, showing where
each coach will stop on the platform, relative to hanging signs
labeled A through E. A passenger's reservation ticket can thus be
matched with the appropriate sign to make it easier to locate one's
seat.

Can you please help me find this coach?
Können Sie mir bitte helfen, diesen Wagen zu finden?
KER-nen zee meer BIT-teh HEL-fen DEE-sen VA-ghen tsoo FIN-den?

Both first and second-class sections on IC trains have restaurant
cars. Some IC trains also come equipped with a buffet car. Some
FD trains and D-Züge also have restaurant or buffet cars. Services
vary on other German trains, but all are clean, comfortable, and
equipped with toilets.

I want a first-class ticket, please.
Ich möchte eine Fahrkarte erster Klasse, bitte.
ikh MERK-teh EYE-neh FAR-kar-teh EHR-ster KLA-seh BIT-teh.

I want an upper berth.
Ich möchte ein Bett oben.
ikh MERK-teh ine BET OH-ben.

I want a lower berth.
Ich möchte ein Bett unten.
ikh MERK-teh ine BET OON-ten.

Where is the washroom?
Wo ist die Toilette?
vo isst dee twa-let-teh?

Is there a restaurant car?
Gibt es einen Speisewagen?
ghibt ess INE-nen SHPY-zeh-va-ghen?

When does service begin for breakfast?
Ab wann wird das Frühstück serviert?
ahb vahn veert dahss FRŮ-stůck zehr-VEERT?

... lunch?
... Mittagessen?
... MIT-tahg-es-sen?

... dinner?
... Abendessen?
... AH-bent-es-sen?

When does service end?
Wann macht der Speisewagen zu?
vahn mahkt dehr SHPY-zeh-va-ghen-tsoo?

Is there a buffet car?
Gibt es einen Zugrestaurant?
ghibt ess EYE-nen TSOOG-res-tau-rahnt?

When is the buffet car open?
Wann ist der Zugrestaurant geöffnet?
vahn isst dehr TSOOG-res-tau-rahnt geh-ERF-net?

Where is the buffet car?
Wo ist der Zugrestaurant?
vo isst dehr TSOOG-res-tau-rahnt?

Can I buy food at this station?
Kann ich Speisen auf diesem Bahnhof kaufen?
kahn ikh SHPY-zen owf DEE-zem BAHN-hohf KOW-fen?

Can I buy something to drink?
Kann ich etwas zu trinken kaufen?
kahn ikh et-VAHS tsoo TRINK-en KOW-fen?

Do I have time to leave the train to buy food?
Habe ich Zeit, den Zug zu verlassen, um etwas zu essen zu kaufen?
HA-beh ikh tzite den tsoog tsoo fair-LA-sen oom ET-vahs tsoo ES-sen tsoo KOW-fen?

Train Fares

Fares on German trains are based on distance, in 10km units for the first 100km; thereafter, in 5km units. Travelers can bypass these increases by purchasing tourist cards (*Touristenkarten*) for 4, 9, or 16 days, for first or second class.

Some IC and FD trains require a supplement (*Zuschlag*) of DM 5 ahead of time or DM 6 for purchase on the train – except when one is traveling on a tourist card. Both the timetable and the platform indicator make clear which trains require a supplement.

How much is this ticket?
Wieviel kostet diese Fahrkarte?
vee-feel KO-stet DEE-seh FAR-kar-teh?

How much would a tourist card cost for 4 days?
Was kostet eine Touristenkarte für vier Tage?
vahss KO-stet INE-neh too-RISS-ten-kar-eh für feer TA-gheh?

... for 9 days?	... for 16 days?
... neun Tage?	**... sechzehn Tage?**
... noyn TA-gheh?	*... ZEK-tsehn TA-gheh?*

Is there a ticket supplement for this train?
Ist dieser Zug zuschlagspflichtig?
isst DEE-zer tsoog TSOO-shlahgs-pflikh-tikh?

Where do I buy the supplement ticket?
Wo kann ich den Zuschlag lösen?
vo kahn ikh dehn tsoo-shlagh LER-zen?

TRAVEL BETWEEN CITIES

Where is the timetable?
Wo ist der Fahrplan?
vo isst dehr FAR-plahn?

BY CAR
German Highways
Driving between cities is extremely easy in Germany, as the network of highways (*Autobahnen*) is extensive and well-maintained. All important cities and towns are on this network, which also connects to international routes.

German highways are all labeled with blue signs, each of which has an *A* (for *Autobahn*) and a number; trans-European highways are marked with a green E and a number.

Where is the highway?
Wo ist die Autobahn?
vo isst dee OW-toh-bahn?

Which route do I take for Munich?
Welche Autobahn muß ich nach München nehmen?
VEL-kheh OWtoh-bahn mooss ikh nahkh mŭn-khen NEH-men?

German highways are extremely busy, and the fast lanes can be very dangerous. Although there are local speed limits that are strictly enforced, there is no general mandatory limit on these national routes. Drivers tend to ignore the recommended limit of 130kmph/80mph, often going as fast as 180kmph/112mph. Driving in Germany is twice as dangerous as it is in the UK or the United States, statistically speaking.

Trucks are banned from German highways on weekends, and even on weekdays, they are never permitted in the fast lane.

Local radio stations regularly broadcast information on traffic conditions, and prominent signs advertise the radio frequencies with this information.

How fast can I go?
Wie schnell kann ich fahren?
vee shnell kahn ikh FA-ren?

Is traffic heavy today?
Ist der Verkehr heute dicht?
isst dehr fair-KEHR HOY-teh dikht?

Which radio station gives traffic information?
Welcher Rundfunksender gibt Verkehrsanweisungen?
VEL-kheh ROOND-foonk-zend-er gibt fehr-KEHRS-ahn-vy-zoon-gen?

Service Stations

Germany's highways are marked with simple rest areas every 5 km–3 miles. Service stations can be found every 30–40km/20–25 miles. Generally, food kiosks can be found at these service areas; often restaurants can be found there as well.

A full tank, please.
Bitte, volltanken!
BIT-teh, fohl-TAHN-ken!

Please clean the windshield.
Bitte machen Sie die Windschutzscheibe sauber!
BIT-teh MA-khen zee dee VINT-shoots-SHY-beh ZOW-ber!

Please check the oil.
Bitte sehen Sie das Öl nach!
BIT-teh ZAY-en zee dahss erl nahkh!

Please check the windshield-wiper fluid.
Bitte kontrollieren Sie die Windschutzscheiben-Flüssigkeit!
BIT-teh kohn-troh-LEE-ren zee dee VINT-shoots-SHY-ben FLÜ-sig-kite!

Please check the tires.
Bitte sehen Sie die Reifen nach!
BIT-teh ZAY-en zee dee RYE-fen nahkh!

Are you a mechanic?
Sind Sie Mechaniker?
zint zee meh-KA-ni-ker?

TRAVEL BETWEEN CITIES

I believe I have a problem with my car.
Ich glaube, ich habe ein Problem mit meinem Wagen.
ikh GLOW-beh ikh HA-beh ine pro-blehm mitt MY-nem VA-ghen.

How far is the next service station?
Wie weit ist die nächste Tankstelle?
vee vite isst dee NEX-teh TAHNK-shtel-leh?

Can I buy food around here?
Kann ich in der Nähe etwas zu essen kaufen?
kahn ikh in dehr NEH-heh ET-vahs tsoo ES-sen KOW-fen?

Where is the next restaurant?
Wo ist das nächste Restaurant?
vo isst dahss NEX-teh res-tau-RAHNT?

Accidents and Breakdowns

If a traveler is involved in an accident on a German highway, he or she should be aware that German law is very clear: someone must be at fault, so the police must make a detailed report in the event of an accident, and they must certainly be called if there is any personal injury or serious damage.

The police can be contacted through emergency phones located every 2km or so along both sides of the *Autobahnen*. A traveler must by law place a warning triangle 150–200m/yd in front of any breakdown or accident – and all cars are required by law to carry such warning triangles. A traveler is also required by law to assist anyone who is injured.

Various German auto clubs operate patrols on main roads, offering assistance in the event of breakdown. Although they will help non-members, they will charge a fee for their services. (For their phone numbers, see "Addresses.")

Can you help me?
Können Sie mir helfen?
KER-nen zee meer HEL-fen?

I have had an accident.
Ich habe einen Unfall gehabt.
ikh HA-beh EYE-nen OON-fahl geh-HABT.

No one is hurt.
Es ist niemand verletzt.
Ess isst NEE-mahnt fair-LETZT.

Someone is hurt.
Jemand ist verletzt.
YAY-mahnt isst fair-LETZT.

Someone is badly hurt.
Jemand ist schwer verletzt.
YAY-mahnt isst shvair fair-LETZT.

It's an emergency!
Es ist ein Notfall!
ess isst ine NOHT-fahl!

My car has broken down.
Ich habe eine Panne.
ikh HAH-be INE-neh PAHN-neh.

Whom should I call for help?
Wen kann ich um Hilfe anrufen?
ven kahn ikh oom HIL-feh AHN-roo-fen?

How do I call the police?
Wie rufe ich die Polizei an?
vee ROO-feh ikh dee PO-lee-tsy ahn?

Parking

Within cities, ordinary roads are decently maintained, but they do not tend to be very fast. Travelers should be aware that on-street parking is very difficult to find in German towns, and garage parking is usually expensive. The emergency number in towns is 110.

TRAVEL BETWEEN CITIES

Where can I find a parking lot?
Wo kann ich einen Parkplatz finden?
vo kann ikh EYE-nen PARK-plats FIN-den?

How much does it cost?
Wieviel wird das kosten?
vee-FEEL veert dahss KO-sten?

How long can I leave my car here?
Wie lange kann ich meinen Wagen hier lassen?
vee LAHN-geh kahn ikh MY-nen VA-ghen here LA-sen?

RELAXATION

BARS

Germany is known for its warm and cordial drinking atmosphere. Travelers will find various types of establishments that serve liquor, each serving its own special purpose. Most bars open at 11.30 a.m. and close at 1 a.m., unless they have a special license to stay open longer.

Hotel bars are generally respectable places where colleagues can be invited for a meeting over drinks, or for a drink to relax after a meeting. Piano and cocktail bars are likewise pleasant and often fashionable places to drink, although they may not be open before 4 p.m.

Where is the hotel bar?
Wo ist die Hotelbar?
vo isst dee ho-TEL-bar?

Is there a good bar in the neighborhood?
Gibt es eine gute Bar in der Nähe?
gibt ess INE-neh GOO-teh bar in dehr NEH-heh?

Will you join me in a drink?
Würden Sie etwas mit mir trinken?
VEER-den zee et-vahs mit meer treen-ken?

What will you have?
Was möchten Sie haben?
vahss MERK-ten zee HA-ben?

Nightclubs may serve liquor, but they are likely to have an entrance fee and to charge quite high prices for drinks. A snack bar is known as an *Imbiß*.

Kneipe is the name of a type of Northern German bar with a cheerful and informal atmosphere and simple furnishings. It is unique in that it is only required to be closed one hour of the twenty-four. Some establishments only close half their premises for this hour; then close the other half the following hour!

Another informal and pleasant type of North German bar is called a *Bierlokal*. To the South, in Bavaria, open air *Biergärten* are especially popular for the beer and music.

No foreign traveler should miss a trip to a local brewery-plus-beer hall, where beer is often served straight from the barrel. These are known as *Brauereikeller* or *Brauerei* everywhere but in Bavaria, where they are known as *Bierkeller*. Likewise, wine growing areas have *Weinstuben*, where travelers can buy wine straight from local vineyards. Cider-producing regions feature *Apfelweinwirtschaften*.

How late is the bar open?
Wie lange ist die Bar geöffnet?
vee LAHN-geh isst dee bar geh-ERF-net?

I'd like a glass of red wine.
Ich möchte ein Glas Rotwein.
ikh MERK-teh ine glahss ROHT-vine.

White wine	cider
Weißwein	**Apfelwein**
VICE-vine	*AHP-fel-vine*
whiskey	brandy
Whiskey	**Cognac**
whisky	*kohn-YAHK*
champagne	mineral water
Sekt	**Mineralwasser**
sekt	*mee-neh-RAHL-va-ser*
tea	coffee
Tee	**Kaffee**
teh	*KA-feh*

I'd like to find a good beer cellar, please.
Ich würde gern einen guten Bierkeller finden.
ikh VÜR-deh-gairn EYE-nen GOO-ten BEER-kel-ler FIN-den.

Where is the best *Weinstube*?
Wo ist die beste Weinstube?
vo ist dee BES-te VINE-shtoo-be?

Can you direct me to an *Apfelweinwirtschaft*?
Können Sie mir sagen, wie ich zu einer Apfelweinwirtschaft komme?
KER-nen zee mere zah-ghen vee ikhtsoo INE-er AHP-fel-vine-VEERT-shahft cohm-meh?

To your health!
Zum Wohl!
tsoom vohl!
or **Prost!**
Prohst!
or (very formally) **Prosit!**

BAR FOOD

Bar food in Germany gives the foreign traveler the chance to sample local snacks, such as Berlin's *Frikadellen* or *Bouletten* (meatballs) or Frankfurt's *Handkäse mit Musik* (cheese, onions, and bread). By law, all establishments must have a printed menu, available to customers to avoid any confusion about prices.

Do you serve food here?
Servieren Sie hier Essen?
zehr-VEE-ren zee here ES-sen?

May I see the menu?
Darf ich die Speisekarte sehen?
darf ikh dee SHPY-zeh-kar-teh ZEH-en?

Can you explain the menu to me?
Können Sie mir die Speisekarte erklären?
KER-nen zee meer dee SHPY-zeh-kar-teh ehr-KLEH-ren?

Do you have an English menu?
Haben Sie eine Speisekarte in englisch?
HA-ben zee EYE-neh SHPY-zeh-kar-teh in ENG-lish?

How much does this cost?
Wieviel kostet das?/Was macht das?
vee-FEEL KO-stet dahss?/vahss makht dahss?

RESTAURANTS

The local hotel or *Gasthof* is probably the restaurant of choice for local businesspeople entertaining the foreign traveler. In the large cities and ports there are a number of excellent international restaurants to choose from.

May I invite you to dinner?
Darf ich Sie zum Abendessen einladen?
darf ikh zee tsoom AH-bent-es-sen INE-la-den?

It would be a pleasure to have dinner with you.
Es würde mir ein Vergnügen sein, mit Ihnen zu speisen.
ess VEER-deh meer ine fairg-Nŭ-ghen zine mitt EE-nen tsoo SHPY-zen.

I would like to invite you and your colleagues to a meal.
Ich möchte Sie und Ihre Kollegen gern zu einer Mahlzeit einladen.
ikh MERKH-teh zee oont EE-reh ko-LEG-en GAIRN tsoo INE-ner MAHL-tsite INE-la-den.

May I invite you and your wife to dinner?
Darf ich Sie und Ihre Frau zum Abendessen einladen?
darf ikh zee oont EE-reh frow-tsoom AH-bent-es-sen INE-la-den?

May I invite you to lunch?
Darf ich Sie zum Mittagessen einladen?
darf ikh zee tsoom MIT-tahk-es-sen INE-la-den?

Can you recommend a good restaurant?
Können sie mir ein gutes Restaurant empfehlen?
KER-nen zee meer ine GOO-tess res-toh-RAHN ehmp-FEH-len?

Most Germans eat lunch sometime between 12:30 and 3. Dinner is served any time after 6.

Reservations are usually necessary for the better restaurants. A morning reservation for that evening is usually sufficient, although longer lead times may be needed for groups of more than four. The traveler who is in a city at the time of a trade fair should be sure to make early reservations, as the dinner hour is likely to be quite crowded.

How late are you open?
Wie lange sind Sie geöffnet?
vee LAHN-geh zint zee geh-ERF-net?

When do you serve lunch?
Wann servieren Sie das Mittagessen?
vahn zehr-VEE-ren zee dahss MIT-tag-es-sen?

How late do you serve dinner?
Wie spät servieren Sie das Abendessen?
vee shpayt sehr-VEE-ren zee dahs AH-bent-es-sen?

I'd like to make a reservation for lunch.
Ich möchte eine Reservierung zum Mittagessen machen.
ikh MERK-teh EYE-neh reh-zer-VEE-roong tsoom MIT-tahk-es-sen MA-khen.

May I make a reservation for dinner?
Darf ich eine Reservierung zum Abendessen machen?
darf ikh EYE-neh reh-zer-VEE-roong tsoom AH-bent-es-sen MA-khen?

There will be —- in our party.
Wir werden —- Personen in unserer Gruppe sein.
veer VEHR-den — pehr-ZO-nen in OON-zer-reh GROO-peh zine.

We have a reservation.
Wir haben eine Reservierung.
veer HA-ben EYE-neh reh-zee-VEE-roong.

I made a reservation this morning.
Ich habe eine Reservierung heute morgen gemacht.
ikh HA-beh EYE-neh reh-zehr-VEE-roong HOY-teh MOR-ghen geh-MAHKT.

RELAXATION

May I smoke?
Darf ich rauchen?
darf ikh RAU-khen?

It was a pleasure to visit your restaurant.
Es war uns eine Freude Ihr Restaurant besucht zu haben.
ess var oonts EYE-neh FROY-deh ear RES-tau-rahnt beh-zookt tsoo HA-ben.

Visitors to some restaurants don't have to wait to be seated, but can simply seat themselves at an empty table and signal to the serving person. A host should say "Good appetite" (*Guten Appetit!*) to guests, and must lift his or her glass to guests before anyone drinks.

Let's sit over there.
Setzen wir uns dort drüben hin.
ZET-zen veer doort DRÜ-ben hin.

Waiter!   Waitress!
Herr Ober!   **Fräulein!**
hair OH-behr!   *FROY-line!*

Good appetite!
Guten Appetit!
GOO-ten ah-peh-TEET!

Restaurants in Germany must display printed menus showing that tax and service are included. Generally, patrons may choose from a fixed-price meal (offering a certain number of courses with a limited choice for each course) or *à la carte* offerings (which change frequently). The better restaurants will offer seasonal dishes. City hotels may offer business lunches that include appetizer, main course, beverage, and perhaps dessert.

As in most European countries, bills in Germany include a service charge. The wine waiter should be tipped in addition; other tips need only be left to show particular appreciation for unusually good service. An additional 5% or a rounding up of the bill usually makes the point. However, no tip should be left for meals served by a restaurant's owner.

May we see the menu?
Dürfen wir die Speisekarte sehen?
dŭr-fen veer dee SHPY-zeh-kar-teh ZEY-hen?

What choices do I have?
Welche Wahl habe ich?
VEL-kheh vahl HA-beh ikh?

Is this à la carte?
Ist das à la carte?
isst dahss a la carte?

What is included in the business lunch?
Was ist in dem Geschäftsmittagessen enthalten?
vahss isst in dem geh-shefts-mit-tahk-es-sen ent-HAHL-ten?

Is the fish fresh today?
Ist der Fisch heute frisch?
isst dehr fish HOY-teh frish?

What do you recommend?
Was schlagen Sie vor?
vahss SHLA-ghen zee for?

I don't understand this bill.
Ich verstehe diese Rechnung nicht.
ikh fair-SHTAY-eh DEE-seh REKH-noong nihkt.

Is this the service charge?
Ist das der Bedienungszuschlag?
isst dahss der beh-DEE-noongs-tsoo-shlagh?

Is that the tax?
Ist das die Steuer?
Isst dahss dee STOY-yer?

Thank you, we enjoyed our meal very much!
Vielen Dank. Das Essen war vorzüglich!
FEE-len dahnk. dahss ES-sen var for-TSŬ-glich!

CULTURAL AND SPORTS EVENTS

Business travelers may enjoy German cultural or sports events, which may have been booked for them by their hosts. If not, the hotel service desk may be very helpful in arranging for tickets, or may be able to recommend a local ticket agency. Tickets to less popular events can be bought at theater box offices or at kiosks in the city center. Opera, ballet, puppet theater, and the circus may be available and of interest to the non-German-speaking visitor. Theater in the former East Germany is undergoing many exciting changes, so for those who wish to brave the language barrier, a visit to a theater or children's theater might be an interesting evening. Sporting events—usually soccer, hockey, and basketball—are popular with foreigners. Foreign-language films in the original language with German subtitles may be available as well.

Are there plays being given in English?
Gibt es Theaterstücke auf english?
gibt ess teh-AH-ter-shtü-keh owf EHNG-lish?

Are there any English-language movies?
Gibt es Filme auf englisch?
gibt ess FEEL-meh owf EHNG-lish?

I'd like to go to the ballet.
Ich würde gern zum Ballett gehen.
ikh VÜR-deh GAIRN ts'oom bal-LEH GEH-en.

What ballets are playing?
Welche Ballette werden aufgeführt?
VEL-kheh ba-LEH-te VAIR-den owf-guh-fürt?

Can we get tickets to the opera?
Können wir Karten für die Oper bekommen?
KER-nen veer KAR-ten für dee O-per beh-KOM-men?

Which operas will be played?
Welche Opern werden gespielt?
VEL-cheh O-pern VAIR-den geh-SHPEELT?

I want tickets to the circus.
Ich möchte Karten für den Zirkus.
ikh MERK-teh KAR-ten für den TSIR-koos.

Can we go to a soccer game?
Können wir zum Fußballspiel gehen?
KER-nen veer tsoom FOOSS-bahl-shpeel GAY-en?

Can we see a hockey game?
Können wir ein Hockeyspiel sehen?
KER-nen veer ine HO-key-shpeel ZAY-en?

Sightseeing can be a pleasure in German cities, if the business traveler has time. As everywhere in the world, it's only courteous to ask permission before taking a photograph of anyone who is not an acquaintance.

I would like to buy some film for this camera.
Ich möchte gern einen Film kaufen für diesen Apparat.
ikh MERK-teh GAIRN EYE-nen FILM KOW-fen fur DEE-zen ah-pa-RAHT.

Can I take your photograph?
Kann ich Sie photographieren?
kahn ikh zee foh-toh-grah-FEE-ren?

Can I take one of you sitting at your desk?
Kann ich ein Foto von Ihnen, an Ihrem Schreibtisch machen?
kahn ikh ine FO-toh fohn EE-nen ahn EE-rem SHRIBE-tish MA-khen?

I would also like to take one of your office staff.
Ich würde gerne eins von Ihren Angestellten machen.
ikh VÜR-deh GAIR-neh ains fohn EE-ren AHN-geh-shtel-ten MA-khen.

I'll send you a copy.
Ich schicke Ihnen einen Abzug.
ikh SHIH-kheh EE-nen INE-nen AHB-tsoog.

MEDICINE AND HEALTH

11

In Germany, health care is private. Although it may be expensive, it reaches very high standards. Medically, Germany is one of the best-equipped countries in the world.

AT THE DOCTOR'S OFFICE

Although doctors' hours are usually 8–12 and 2–6, a medical office will always have a doctor on call 24 hours a day, as well as a receptionist and a nurse permanently on duty. For a high fee, a doctor can come to a traveler's hotel room.

I want to locate a doctor.
Ich möchte einen Arzt aufsuchen.
ich MERK-teh EYE-nen artst auf-ZOO-khen.

My throat hurts.
Ich habe Halsweh.
ikh HA-beh HAHLS-veh.

My head hurts.
Mein Kopf tut weh.
mine kopf toot vay.

My stomach hurts.
Ich habe Bauchschmerzen.
ikh HA-beh BOWKH-shmehrt-sen.

My arm hurts.
Mein Arm tut weh.
mine arm toot vay.

My leg hurts.
Mein Bein tut weh.
mine bine toot vay.

Do I have a fever?
Habe ich Fieber?
HA-beh ikh FEE-ber?

Can you prescribe something for a headache?
Können Sie mir etwas für Kopschmerzen verschreiben?
KER-nen zee meer ET-vahss für KOHPF-shmehrt-sen
fair-SHRY-ben?

....a cold?
....eine Erkältung?
... EYE-neh ehr-KEL-toong?

...an upset stomach?
...gegen Magenschmerzen?
... GAY-ghen MAH-ghen-shmehrt-sen?

I have high blood pressure.
Ich habe hohen Blutdruck.
ikh HA-beh HO-hen BLOOT-drook.

I have a heart problem.
Ich habe Herzbeschwerden.
ikh HA-beh HAIRTZ-beh-SHVER-den.

PHARMACIES
Of course, some medicine is available without prescription, and every German city district has at least one 24-hour drugstore. Finding that establishment can be done through a hotel, the local paper, or the police. In addition, every pharmacy with shorter hours will display information on where the 24-hour drugstores are.

I need some medicine.
Ich brauche Medikamente.
ikh BROW-keh meh-dee-ka-MEN-teh.

Where is the nearest drugstore?
Wo ist die nächste Apotheke?
vo isst dee NEX-teh ah-po-TEK-eh?

Do I need a prescription for this medicine?
Brauche ich ein Rezept für dieses Medikament?
BROW-keh ikh ine reh-tsept für DEE-ses meh-dee-kah-MENT?

DOCTORS' LETTERS

Travelers with particular health problems should bring letters from their doctors outlining their medical histories and treatment. If at all possible, this letter should be translated into German before leaving home. Such a letter might also facilitate going through customs with medications and syringes.

Here is letter from my doctor.
Hier ist ein Brief von meinem Arzt.
here isst ine breef von MY-nem artzt.

Do you understand English?
Verstehen Sie englisch?
fer-shteh-en zee ENG-lish?

I have a letter in English describing my medical history.
Ich habe einen Brief in englisch der meine Krankengeschichte beschreibt.
ikh HA-beh EYE-nen breef in ENG-lish dehr MY-neh KRAHN-ken-gay-shikh-teh beh-SHRYBT.

EMERGENCY TREATMENT

Emergency treatment is available through the emergency rooms of local hospitals. Any taxi driver will be able to take a traveler there. In case of extreme emergency, a traveler can call police by dialing 110 or by pulling the lever beside the phone in some phone booths.

To the hospital, please!
Zum Krankenhaus, bitte!
tsoom KRAHN-ken-house, BIT-teh!

It's an emergency!
Das ist ein Notfall!
dahss isst ine NOTE-fahl!

Where is the nearest emergency room?
Wo ist die nächste Unfallstation?
vo isst die NEX-teh OON-fahl-sta-ts'yohn?

I have to call a hospital.
Ich muß das Krankenhaus anrufen.
ikh moose dahss KRAHN-ken-house AHN-roo-fen.

Where's a phone?
Wo gibt es ein Telefon?
vo gibt ess ine teh-leh-FOHN?

I must go to the hospital.
ich muß zum Krankenhaus.
ikh moose tsoom KRAHN-ken-house.

Where is the taxi stand?
Wo ist der Taxistand?
vo isst dehr TAHK-see-shtant?

AT THE DENTIST

Dental treatment in Germany is extremely expensive, since it is all provided privately. However, in case of emergency, travelers can be sure of finding a 24-hour dentist in every large town. Once again, the hotel, the police, and the local newspaper should make this information available.

I need a dentist.
Ich brauche einen Zahnarzt.
ikh BROW-kheh EYE-nen TSAHN-artz.

Where can I find a dentist?
Wo kann ich einen Zahnarzt finden?
vo kahn ikh EYE-nen TSAHN-artzt FIN-den?

My tooth hurts.
Mein Zahn tut weh.
mine tsahn toot vay.

I've chipped a tooth.
Ich habe ein Stück Zahn verloren.
ikh HA-beh ine shtŭk tsahn fair-LO-ren.

I've lost a filling.
Ich habe eine Plombe verloren.
ikh HA-beh EYE-neh PLOM-beh FEHR-lo-ren.

HEALTH INSURANCE

Travelers concerned about their health might research their insurance before leaving home, as many countries have reciprocal health care arrangements with Germany. In those cases, treatment costs may be greatly reduced or even free. Even so, reimbursement may take a long time, so travelers may want to take out insurance to cover the cost of medical emergencies, including the expense of returning home unexpectedly.

Here is my insurance form.
Hier ist meine Versicherungskarte.
here isst MY-neh fair-ZIKH-er-oongs-KAR-teh.

Can you help me fill out this form?
Können Sie mir beim Ausfüllen des Formulars helfen?
KER-nen zee meer bime OWSS-füll-en dess fohr-moo-lahrs HEL-fen?

Where should I pay?
Wo muß ich bezahlen?
vo moose ikh beh-TZAL-len?

How much do I owe you?
Wieviel bin ich schuldig?
vee-FEEL bin ikh SHOOL-dig?

GENERAL PHRASES

Business travelers who need to see medical personnel will find them courteous and helpful. Naturally, an interpreter should be used to communicate with anyone not fluent in English, but using a few phrases in German may also help create a friendly, cordial atmosphere.

Thank you for your trouble
Vielen Dank für Ihre Mühe.
FEE-len dahnk für EEH-reh Mü-heh.

When should I come back?
Wann muß ich wiederkommen?
vahn moose ikh VEE-dehr-ko-men?

DAILY LIFE

12

FINDING GOODS AND SERVICES YOU NEED

Foreign travelers to most parts of Germany are likely to find the goods, services, and products with which they're familiar. Even in the former German Democratic Republic (GDR or East Germany), the quality and availability of goods and services is comparable to the West.

For the foreign traveler, then, the problem is not the availability of goods and services, but the finding of them. Generally, hotel personnel are happy to assist with locating services that they themselves do not provide. Travelers may find that the more expensive international hotels offer services that are available more cheaply elsewhere; however, hotel personnel will usually be happy to help locate even those services that they themselves offer.

Where can I get my laundry done?
Wo kann ich meine Wäsche waschen lassen?
vo kahn ikh MY-neh VEH-sheh VA-shen LA-sen?

When is laundry picked up?
Wann wird die Wäsche abgeholt?
vahn veert dee VEH-sheh AHB-geh-holt?

When will my laundry be ready?
Wann wird meine Wäsche fertig sein?
vahn veert MY-neh VEH-sheh FAIR-tikh zine?

What time can I pick it up?
Wann kann ich sie abholen?
vahn kahn ikh zee ahb-HO-len?

Can you deliver my laundry to my room for me?
Können Sie meine Wäsche zu meinem Zimmer bringen?
KER-nen zee MY-neh VEH-sheh tsoo MY-nem TSIM-mer BRING-en?

Where can I get my things dry-cleaned?
Wo kann ich meine Sachen reinigen lassen?
vo kahn ikh MY-neh ZAK-hen RYE-nee-ghen LA-sen?

How long does dry-cleaning take?
Wie lange dauert die Reinigung?
vee LAHN-geh DOW-ert dee RYE-nee-goong?

Do you have dry-cleaning express service?
Haben Sie Expreßreinigung?
HA-ben zee express-rye-nee-goong?

I need to buy some toilet articles.
Ich möchte ein paar Toilettenartikel kaufen.
ikh MERK-ter ine par twa-LET-ten-AR-tee-kel KOW-fen.

Where should I go?
Wo soll ich hingehen?
vo zoll ikh hin-geh-en?

I must buy toothpaste.
Ich muß Zahnpasta kaufen.
ikh mooss TSAHN pa-sta KOW-fen.

...dental floss.
... Zahnseide.
...TSAHN-zy-deh

... deodorant.
... Deodorant.
... deh-o-doh-RAHNT.

...shampoo.
... Haarwaschmittel.
... HAR-wahsh-mit-tel.

... conditioner.
... Pflegespülung.
...PLFEH-ghe-shpü-loong.

... hand lotion.
... Handcreme.
... HAHNT-krehme.

... shaving lotion.
... Rasierschaum.
... ra-ZEER-showm.

... Kleenex.
... Tempos.
... TEM-pohs.

... aspirin.
... Aspirin.
... AH-speh-rin.

... Tampons.
... Tampons.
... TAHM-pohnz.

I have to buy a toothbrush.
Ich möchte eine Zahnbürste kaufen.
ikh MERK-teh EYE-neh TSAHN-bůr-steh KOW-fen.

... shower cap.
... eine Duschhaube.
... EYE-neh DOOSH-how-beh.

... a razor.
... einen Rasierer.
... EYE-nen ra-ZEE-rehr.

... a bathing suit.
... einen Badeanzug.
... EYE-nen BA-deh-ahn-tsoog.

... a bathing cap.
... eine Badekappe.
... EYE-neh BA-de-KA-peh.

Where can I get my shoes shined?
Wo kann ich meine Schuhe putzen lassen?
vo kahn ikh MY-neh SHOO-heh PUT-zen LA-sen?

Where can I get these shoes repaired?
Wo kann ich diese Schuhe reparieren lassen?
vo kahn ikh DEE-zeh SHOO-heh reh-pa-REER-en LA-sen?

How long will it take?
Wie lange wird es dauern?
vee LAHN-geh veert ess DOW-ern?

SHOPPING
Generally, shopping hours in Germany are from 9 a.m. to 6.30 p.m.
Monday to Friday, although these hours may vary from region to
region. Smaller towns may shut down at lunchtime – from 1 p.m.
to 3 p.m. Throughout Germany, shops are generally open on
Saturday mornings but closed by 1 or 2 in the afternoon and all day
Sunday, although the first Saturday in the month is usually an occa-
sion for stores to remain open until 4 p.m. or 5 p.m.

How late are you open?
Wie lange sind Sie geöffnet?
vee LAHN-geh zint zee geh-ERF-net?

Are you closed for lunch?
Sind Sie zum Mittagessen geschlossen?
zint zee tsoom MIT-tahg-ES-sen geh-SHLO-sen?

Will you be open tomorrow?
Sind Sie morgen geöffnet?
Zint zee MOR-ghen geh-ERF-net?

Is any store still open?
Gibt es noch ein Geschäft, das geöffnet ist?
gibt ess nohkh ine geh-SHEFT dahs geh-ERF-net isst?

I must buy something.
Ich muß etwas kaufen.
ikh moose ET-vahss KOW-fen.

The current Value Added Tax, or sales tax (*Mehrwertsteuer*) in Germany is 14%, although food products and other specified items are only charged at the rate of 7%. Travelers who save their receipts may be able to reclaim this tax at customs.

How much does this cost?
Wieviel kostet das?
vee-FEEL ko-STET dahss?

Could I have a receipt?
Darf ich um eine Quitting bitten?
darf ikh oom EYE-neh KVEE-toong BIT-en?

CLIMATE

Spring and fall are perhaps the most pleasant times to visit Germany. Whatever the season, however, the temperate, mild German climate poses few difficulties for the foreign traveler. A visitor to Germany should bring warm clothes in winter, as well as a raincoat, whatever the season.

German winters can be cold and wet, with daytime temperatures averaging around 35°F (1.5°C) in the southern lowlands and 18°F (–6°C) in the Bavarian Alps. Frost is common in the lowlands; heavy snowfalls are frequent in the mountains. Northern Germany features milder winter temperatures, but more rain.

Summers likewise feature moderate temperatures: an average July high of 62°F (17°C) in the northern lowlands; a comparable 70°F (20°C) in the southern valleys. The cooler north also sees more changeable and less sunny weather.

CRIME

Crime is a problem only in certain areas of large cities in Germany. However, travelers – particularly those unfamiliar with a city – should certainly take standard precautions: carry wallets in inside jacket pockets; carry bags close to the body; avoid carrying cash; and store valuables in the hotel safe. Avoid unlit streets and empty train compartments; walk in the middle of the street if necessary.

Does this hotel have a safe?
Hat dieses Hotel einen Safe?
haht DEE-zes ho-TEL EYE-nen safe?

May I leave this with you?
Kann ich das hierlassen?
Kahn ikh dahss HERE-la-sen?

Here is where I am going.
Hier gehe ich hin.
here GAY-heh ikh hin.

Is that a safe part of town?
Ist das ein sicherer Stadtteil?
isst dahss ine ZICK-er-er shtaht-tile?

Foreign travelers to Germany should always remember to lock their cars; in fact, they may be fined if they do not! No baggage should ever be left visible inside a car, nor should car documents be stored there.

Any robberies should be reported to the police immediately, either by dialing the 110 emergency number or by going to the nearest police station. Of course, an embassy can help replace a lost passport; travel agencies can restore lost tickets (sometimes at a price); and banks or credit agencies can replace lost credit cards or travelers checks.

I've been robbed!
Ich bin beraubt worden!
ikh bin beh-ROWBT VOR-den!

Where is the police station?
Wo ist die Polizeiwache?
vo isst dee po-lee-TSY-va-kheh?

How can I replace my credit card?
Wie kann ich meine Kreditkarte ersetzen?
vee kahn ikh MY-neh kreh-dit-KAR-teh ehr-ZET-sen?

... my traveler's checks?	... my airline ticket?
... meine Reiseschecks?	**... meinen Flugschein?**
... MY-neh RYE-zeh-shecks?	*... MY-nen FLOOG-shine?*

.... my passport?	... my railway ticket?
... meinen Paß?	**... meine Bahnfahrkarte?**
... MY-nen pahss?	*... MY-neh bahn-FAR-kar-teh?*

In the very unlikely event that a foreign business traveler should be arrested, it is important that you know your rights. An interpreter should be provided at a traveler's request. Travelers should also be told the reason for their arrest, given the right to call a friend or a lawyer, and told that anything they say may be used against them. A lawyer should be on duty at the police station to advise foreign travelers (as well as German citizens, of course). The police are not allowed to hold anyone for more than 24 hours without charging them with a specific crime.

However, in the case of terrorist activity, all persons within German borders are legally required to give police any information that they have. Also, in such cases the police may hold a person for more than 24 hours.

I would like an interpreter, please.
Ich hätte gern einen Dolmetscher.
ikh HET-teh gairn EYEnen DOHL-met-cher.

May I make a phone call?
Darf ich einen Anruf machen?
Darf ikh EYE-nen AHN-roof MA-khen?

I don't understand these charges.
Ich verstehe diese Beschuldigungen nicht.
ikh FAIR-shtay-eh DEE-zeh beh-SHOOL-dee-gung-en nihkt.

I would like to wait for my lawyer.
Ich möchte auf meinen Rechtsanwalt warten.
ikh MERK-teh owf MY-nen rekts-AHN-wahlt VAR-ten.

I would like to call the American Consulate.
Ich möchte das amerikanische Konsulat anrufen.
ikh MERK-teh dahss ah-MEH-ree-kah-nee-sheh kohn-soo-LAHT AHN-roo-fen

... to call the British Consulate.
... das britische Konsulat anrufen.
... dahss BRIH-tish-eh kohn-soo-LAHT AHN-roo-fen.

...to call the Canadian Consulate
... das kanadische Konsulat anrufen.
... dahss ka-NA-dis-sheh kohn-soo-LAHT AHN-roo-fen.

ADDRESSES

TOURIST INFORMATION

Munich-Information
Sonnenstraße 10
W-8000 München 2
Tel.: 089/597347

Hamburg-Information GmbH
Neuer Jungfernstieg 5
W-2000 Hamburg 36
Tel.: 040/351301

Frankfurt-Information
Karl-Marx-Straße 8a
0-1200 Frankfurt/Oder
Tel.: 030/22249

Leipzig-Information
Sachsenplatz
0-7010 Leipzig
Tel.: 041/79590

Cologne-Information
Unter Fettenhennen 19
50668 Köln
Tel.: 221/2213345

Düsseldorf-Information
Immermannstraße 65b
Ecke Konrad-Adenauer-Platz
40213 Düsseldorf
Tel.: 211/350505

Bonn-Information
Niebuhrstraße 16b
W-5300 Bonn 1
Tel.: 228/214071–73

ADDRESSES

Berlin-Information
Europa-Centre
W-1000 Berlin 30
Tel.: 030/21234

STATE ECONOMIC AGENCIES

Bayernsches Staatsministerium (Bavaria)
Prinzregentenstraße 28
D-8000 München 22
Tel.: 89/2162-2642
Fax: 89/2162-2760

**Hamburgische Gesellschaft für
Wirtschaftsförderung mbH-HWF (Hamburg)**
Hamburger Straße 1
D-2000 Hamburg 76
Tel.: 40/227019-0
Fax: 40/227019-29

**Wirtschaftsförderung Hessen
Investitionsbank AG (Hesse)**
Abraham-Lincoln-Straße 38–42
D-6200 Wiesbaden
Tel.: 611/774-0
Fax: 611/774-265

**Gesellschaft für
Wirtschaftsforderung Nordrhein-Westfalen mbh
(North Rhine—Westphalia)**
Kavalleriestraße 8–10
D-4000 Düsseldorf I
Tel.: 211/13000-0
Fax: 211/13000-54

Wirtschaftsförderung
Sachsen Gmbh (Saxony)
Albertstraße 34
D-8060 Dresden
Tel.: 351/5022981-86
Fax: 351/5023030

EMBASSIES

USA
Deichmanns Ave
5300 Bonn 2
Tel.: 228/339-1

Great Britain
Friedrich-Ebert-Allee 77
5300 Bonn 1
Tel.: 228/344061

Canada
Friedrich-Wilhelm-Straße 18
5300 Bonn 1
Tel.: 228/231061

CHAMBERS OF COMMERCE

Leipzig
Industrie- und Handelskammer zu Leipzig
Goerdelerring 5
04109 Leipzig
Tel.: 0341/71530
Fax: 0341/7153421

ADDRESSES

Düsseldorf
Industrie- und Handelskammer zu Düsseldorf
Postfach 101017
Ernst-Schneider-Platz 1
40212 Düsseldorf 1
Tel.: 0211/35570
Fax: 0211/3557400

Munich
Industrie- und Handelskammer für München und Oberbayern
letters:
Postfach 8000
München 34

Max-Joseph-Straße 2
80333 München 2
Tel.: 089/5116-0
Fax: 089/5116-306

Cologne
Industrie- und Handelskammer zu Köln
Postfach 108015
Unter Sachsenhausen 10–26
50667 Köln 1
Tel.: 221/16400
Fax: 221/1640123

Hamburg
Handelskammer Hamburg
Postfach 111449
Börse
20457 Hamburg 11
Tel.: 40/361380
Fax: 40/36138401

Frankfurt am Main
Industrie- und Handelskammer Frankfurt am Main
Postfach 101139
Börsenplatz
60313 Frankfurt am Main 1
Tel.: 69/21970
Fax: 69/2197-424

Berlin
Industrie- und Handelskammer zu Berlin
Hardenbergstraße 16–18
W-1000 Berlin 12
Tel.: 30/315100
Fax: 30/31510316

Bonn
Industrie- und Handelskammer zu Bonn
Bonner Talweg 17
W-530 Bonn 1
Tel.: 228/22840
Fax: 228/2284170

USEFUL RESOURCES (TELEPHONE NUMBERS)

AIR TRAVEL
Lufthansa (reservations)

Frankfurt	69/255255
Hamburg	40/359255
Munich	089/545599
Cologne	221/920820
Düsseldorf	0211/8688100
Berlin	30/8875088
Leipzig	341/1299952

AUTOMOBILE ASSISTANCE
Allgemeiner Deutscher Automobil-Club (ADAC):
089/76760

Emergency:
110

CAR RENTAL
Avis	069/730505
Budget/Sixt	089/791071
Hertz	069/730404

INFORMATION SOURCES

Ausstellungs- und Messe-Ausschuß der Deutschen Wirtschaft e.V. (AUMA) — The Confederation of German Trade Fair and Exhibition Industries
Lindenstraße 8
D-5000 Köln 1
Tel.: 0221/209070

Publications:
Messehandbuch, a handbook published twice a year in five languages listing every German trade fair, with program information up to three years in advance.
Information Guide, an English publication giving suggestions for taking part in trade fairs, as well as statistical information.

Bundesverband der Deutschen Industrie (BDI) — Federation of German Industry
Gustav-Heinemann–Ufer 84–88
Postfach 51048
D-5000 Köln 51
Tel.: 0221/370800

Publications:
Made in Germany, gives information on Germany's economy as well as presenting *Internationale Wirtschaftszahlen* (international economic indicators).

**Deutscher Industrie- und Handelstag (DIHT) —
Federation of German Chambers of Commerce**
Adenauerallee 148
D-5300 Bonn 1
Tel.: 0228/104186

Publications:
A booklet listing all overseas offices of German Chambers of
Commerce.

**Zentralverband Elektrotechnik- und Elektronikindustrie e.V. (ZVEI) —
German Electrical and Electronics Manufacturers Association**
Stresemannallee 19
D-600 Frankfurt am Main 70
Tel.: 069/63021

Publications:
Taschenbuch der Elektropresse, a directory of manufacturers of
new technology.
Elektro-Elektronik Einkaufs-Führer, the annual ZVEI buying guide.

GRAMMAR: AN INTRODUCTION

14

English-speaking people have a distinct advantage when learning to speak German since so many words closely resemble their counterparts in the other tongue. With a slight change in pronunciation or spelling they become mutually understandable, and even the long German words become recognizable when they are broken down in to their component parts.

Certain important differences in writing, spelling, and pronunciation should be remembered:

- All German nouns begin with a capital letter.
- The gender of each noun is indicated in this word list by the word for "the." This word is *der*, *die*, or *das*, which indicates, in the above order, whether the noun is grammatically masculine, feminine, or neuter.
- The plural of most nouns is not written with an "s," but ends with -n, -en, -e, or -er and often a slight change in the noun's basic spelling.

German uses case endings for adjectives and some nouns according to whether the adjective precedes or follows a noun as predicate.

e.g.: the brown cow   die braune Kuh
     the cow is brown   die Kuh ist braun

In the word list the predicate adjective is given first and the adjective endings -er, -e, -es, second.

The predicate adjective can also be used as an adverb:

    She sings beautifully   Sie singt schön
    She is beautiful   Sie ist schön

There are four cases, indicated by case endings where applicable. These cases are nominative (subject of a sentence), genitive (indicating possession), accusative (object of a verb), and dative (indirect object and with prepositions of location). Case endings for the article and other adjectives are as follows:

Singular   **Plural** (*for all three genders*)
Nominative: der, die, das   die
Genitive: des, der, des   der
Accusative: den, die, das   die
Dative: dem, der, dem   den

Case endings for pronouns I, me, my, etc. are included within the word list itself.

The future tense is formed by combining the present tense of *werden* (to become) with the infinitive.

I will go	ich werde gehen
he, she, it, will go	er, sie, es wird gehen
we, you, they will go	wir, Sie, sie werden gehen

and the negative:

I won't go – ich werde *nicht* gehen

The perfect tense (generally used for past action) is formed with the past participle combined with the present form of *haben* or *sein*:

The past participle closely resembles the infinitive but is generally preceded by *ge-* and ends with *-t* or *-n*.

English	**German infinitive**	**Past participle** (Using *haben* or *sein*)
I take	nehmen	ich habe genommen
I eat	essen	ich habe gegessen
I open	öffnen	ich habe geöffnet
I say	sagen	ich habe gesagt
I find	finden	ich habe gefunden
I drink	trinken	ich habe getrunken
I speak	sprechen	ich habe gesprochen
I make	machen	ich habe gemacht
I hear	hören	ich habe gehört
I am	sein	ich bin gewesen
I go	gehen	ich bin gegangen

For the imperative: Take the infinitive form of the verb and follow it with *Sie* (you).

Come! – Kommen Sie!

In the preceding chapters you have been given, on the third line of each insert, a close English sound of the German sentence. In the following word list we offer the pronunciation of certain letters and how they sound when written within a word. This short list will reinforce your pronunciation of the words you have already learned in this book, and any new words you may see on signs or in newspapers, business and other reports, magazines, or anything written in German.

PRONUNCIATION POINTS TO REMEMBER

German letter or letter combinations	English equivalent
a	ah
ä	eh
au	ow
b	b (but p at end of syllable)
ch	kh (as in Bach)
d	d (but t at end of syllable)
e	eh
ei	eye
eu	oy
g	hard g, generally sounding like k at end of syllable or word
i	ee, ih
ie	ee
j	y
ö	er
qu	kv
s	z at beginning or within a word, s at end of word.
ß	ss
sp	shp at beginning of word
sch	sh
th	t
u	oo
ü	say ee with pursed lips.*
v	f
w	v
z	ts

*In the phonetic pronunciation used in this book the ü is expressed by ů.

A BUSINESS DICTIONARY

15

a (or) one	**ein (m,n) eine (f)**
accident	**(der) Unfall**
account	**(des) Konto**
address	**(die) Adresse**
advertising	**(die) Reklame**
afternoon	**(der) Nachmittag**
Africa	**Afrika**
African (person)	**(der) Afrikaner (m)**
	(die) Afrikanerin (f)
again	**noch einmal**
agent	**(der) Vertreter**
	(die) Vertretung
agency	**(der) Agent**
(to) agree	**zustimmen**
agreement	**(die) Zustimmung**
air conditioner	**(die) Klimaanlage**
air mail	**(die) Luftpost**
airplane	**(das) Flugzeug**
airport	**(der) Flughafen**
all	**alle**
(to) allow	**erlauben**
also	**auch**
America	**Amerika**
American *n.*	**Amerikaner (m)**
American *adj.*	**amerikanisch (-er, -e, -es)**
and	**und**
answer	**(die) Antwort**
antique/antiques	**antik *adj.*/(die) Antiquität (-en)**
appointment	**(die) Verabredung**
	(der) Termin
April	**(der) April**
Arab *n.*	**Araber (m)**
	Araberin (f)
Arabic *adj.* and *lang.*	**arabisch**
(to) arrange	**planen**
(to) arrive	**ankommen**
art	**(die) Kunst**
Asia	**Asien**
Asian (person)	**Asiate (m)**
	Asiatin (f)
(to) ask	**fragen**
at	**um, in, bei**
Atlantic Ocean	**(der) Atlantische Ozean**
attorney	**(der) Rechtsanwalt**
August	**(der) August**
Australia	**Australien**

Australian *n.*	**Australier (m)**
	Australierin (f)
Austria	**Österreich**
Austrian	**Österreicher (m)**
	Österreicherin (f)
automobile	**(das) Automobil**
bad	**schlecht**
bag	**(der) koffer**
	(die) Tasche
baggage	**(das) Gepäck**
balance	**(der) Saldo**
bank	**(die) Bank**
bank account	**(das) Bankkonto**
bank draft	**(die) Tratte**
banker	**(der) Bankier**
basis	**(die) Basis**
beautiful	**schön**
(to) be	**sein**
beer	**(das) Bier**
best	**beste (-er, -e, -es)** *adj.*/**am besten** *adv.*
better	**besser**
big	**groß**
bill	**(die) Rechnung**
black	**schwarz**
blue	**blau**
boat	**(das) Boot**
book	**(das) Buch**
(to) borrow	**borgen**
box	**(die) Schachtel**
Brazil	**Brasilien**
Brazilian *n.*	**Brasilianer (m)**
	Brasilianerin (f)
Brazilian *adj.*	**brazilianisch**
broken	**zerbrochen**
brown	**braun**
build	**bauen**
building	**(das) Gebäude**
bus	**(der) Bus**
business	**(das) Geschäft**
businessman	**(der) Geschäftsmann**
busy	**besetzt**
but	**aber**
(to) buy	**kaufen**
calculator	**(der) Kalkulator**

camera	(der) Fotoapparat
can (container)	(die) Büchse/(die) Dose
can (to be able)	können
Canada	Kanada
Canadian *n.*	Kanadier (m)/
	Kanadierin (f)
Canadian *adj.*	kanadisch (-er, -e, -es)
(to) cancel	abbestellen
can (container)	(die) Büchse/(die) Dose
can (to be able)	können
capital (money)	(das) Kapital
car	(der) Wagen/(das) Auto
careful	vorsichtig
cash	(das) Bargeld
cassette	(die) Kassette
cassette tape	(das) Tonband
catalog	(der) Katalog
certainly	natürlich
certified check	(der) bestätigte(r) Scheck
cheap	billig
check (bank)	(der) Scheck
chemicals	(die) Chemikalien
China	china
Chinese (person)	chineser (m)
	chinesin (f)
Chinese (adj. and lang.)	chinesisch (-er, -e, -es)
(to) choose	wählen
C.I.F.	Kosten, Versicherung, Fracht
coffee	(der) Kaffee
commission	(die) Provision
company	(die) Gesellschaft
compensation	(die) Entschädigung
competition	(die) Konkurrenz
consignment	(die) Sendung
contingency	(die) Eventualität
contract	(der) Vertrag
(to) cooperate	zusammenarbeiten
copy	(die) Kopie
customer	(der) Kunde (m)
	(die) Kundin (f)
customs (tax)	(der) Zoll
damaged	beschädigt
dangerous	gefährlich
date	(das) Datum
day	(der) Tag
December	(der) Dezember

delicious	**delikat/Schmackhaft**
(to) deliver	**(aus)liefern**
(to) demonstrate	**demonstrieren**
(to) depart	**abfahren**
department store	**(das) Kaufhaus**
deposit	**(die) Anzahlung**
(to) develop	**entwickeln**
diesel engine	**(der) Dieselmotor**
different	**verschieden/unterschiedlich**
difficult	**schwer (-er, -e, -es)**
difficulty	**Schwierigkeit**
dinner	**(das) Abendessen**
direction	**(die) Richtung**
discount	**(der) Rabatt**
distributor	**(der) Verteiler**
distribution	**(die) Verteilung**
do	**tun**
don't forget!	**nicht vergessen!**
dollar	**(der) Dollar**
dress	**(das) Kleid**
driver	**(der) Fahrer**
drugstore	**(die) Apotheke**
duty free	**zollfrei**
each	**jeder, jede, jedes**
earth	**(die) Erde**
east	**(der) Osten**
easy	**leicht -er, -e, -es**
economy	**(die) Wirtschaft (slage)**
efficient	**effizient/wirkungsvoll**
eight	**acht**
eighteen	**achtzehn**
eighty	**achtzig**
electricity	**(die) Elektrizität**
eleven	**elf**
embassy	**(die) Botschaft**
emergency	**(der) Notfall**
England	**England**
English (person)	**(der) Engländer (m)**
	(die) Engländerin (f)
English (adj. and lang.)	**englisch (-er, -e, -es)**
enough	**genug**
entrance	**(der) Eingang**
equipment	**(die) Ausrüstung/Einrichtung**
Europe	**Europa**
evening	**(der) Abend**

exchange rate	(der) Wechselkurs
exhibition	(die) Ausstellung / Messe
exit	(der) Ausgang
(to) expedite	beschleunigen
expense	(die) Ausgabe
expensive	teuer (-er, e, -es)
experience *n.*	(die) Erfahrung
(to) explain	erklären
export	(die) Ausfuhr/(der) Export
(to) export	exportieren
(by) express mail	(per) Eilbote/Eilbrief
fabric	(der) Stoff
face *n.*	(das) Gesicht
factory	(die) Fabrik
famous	berühmt
fashion	(die) Mode
fast (quick)	schnell
February	(der) Februar
film (for camera)	(der) Film
film (movie)	(der) Film
fifteen	fünfzehn
fifty	fünfzig
final offer	letztes Angebot
final payment	letzte Zahlung
(to) finish	beenden
firm offer	festes Angebot
five	fünf
flight (aircraft)	(der) Flug
food	(das) Essen
forbidden	verboten
foreign exchange	(die) Devisen
foreign exchange market	(der) Devisenmarkt
foreigner	(der) Ausländer (m)
	(die) Ausländerin (f)
forty	vierzig
four	vier
fourteen	vierzehn
France	Frankreich
free (no cost)	gratis
freight	(die) Fracht
French (person)	(der) Franzose (m)
	(die) Französin (f)
French (adj. and lang.)	französisch (-er, -e, -es)
Friday	Freitag
friend	(der) Freund (m)

	(die) Freundin (f)
friendship	**(die) Freundschaft**
from	**von, aus**
fur	**(der) Pelz**
furniture	**(die) Möbel (pl.)**
garage	**(die) Garage/(die) Werkstatt**
gasoline	**(das) Benzin**
gas station	**(die) Tankstelle**
German *n*.	**(ein) Deutscher (m)**
	(eine) Deutsche (f)
German (adj. and lang.)	**deutsch (-er, -e, -es)**
Germany	**Deutschland**
(to) give	**geben**
glad	**froh**
glass	**(das) Glas**
go	**gehen**
gold	**(das) Gold**
(made of) gold	**aus Gold**
goodbye	**auf Wiedersehen**
good morning	**guten Morgen!**
good evening	**guten Abend!**
government	**(die) Regierung**
Greece	**Griechenland**
Greek (adj. and lang.)	**griechisch (-er, -e, -es)**
green	**grün**
(to) guarantee	**garantieren**
guest	**(der) Gast**
guide	**(der) Fremdenführer**
guidebook	**(der) Reiseführer**
handbag	**(die) Handtasche**
half	**(die) Hälfte**
he	**er**
headquarters	**(die) Zentrale/(der) Hauptsitz**
(to) hear	**hören**
heavy	**schwer**
(to) help	**helfen**
her (object)	**sie**
(possessive)	**ihr**
here	**hier**
high	**hoch**
him/to him	**ihn/ihm**
hire	**anstellen/mieten**
his	**sein**
holiday	**(der) Feiertag/(die) Ferien**

hospital	**(das) Krankenhaus**
host	**(der) Gastgeber**
hostess	**(die) Gastgeberin**
hotel	**(das) Hotel**
hour	**(die) Uhr**
how	**wie**
how are you?	**wie geht es Ihnen?**
how far is it?	**wie weit ist es?**
how long? (time)	**wie lange?**
how much?	**wieviel?**
hundred	**hundert**
hundred thousand	**hundert tausend**
Hungary	**Ungarn**
Hungarian *n.*	**Ungare (m)**
	Ungarin (f)
Hungarian (adj. and lang.)	**ungarisch (-er, -e, -es)**
(to) hurry	**sich beeilen**
hurry up!	**beeilen Sie sich!**
husband	**(der) Gatte/Ehemann**
ice	**(das) Eis**
if	**wenn, ob**
immediately	**sofort**
(to) import	**importieren**
import license	**(die) Einfuhrlizenz**
important	**wichtig**
impossible	**unmöglich**
in, into	**in**
income	**(das) Einkommen**
income tax	**(die) Einkommenssteuer**
India	**Indien**
Indian *n.*	**Inder (m)**
	Inderin (f)
industry	**(die) Industrie**
inexpensive	**preiswert**
information	**(die) Auskunft**
injury	**(die) Verletzung**
(to) insist	**bestehen**
(to) inspect	**besichtigen**
inspection	**(die) Besichtigung**
installment	**(die) Abzahlung**
insurance	**(die) Versicherung**
interest (financial)	**(die) Zinsen (pl.)**
interpreter	**(der) Dolmetscher (m)**
	(die) Dolmetscherin (f)

A BUSINESS DICTIONARY

(to) invest	**investieren**
invoice	**(die) Rechnung**
Ireland	**Irland**
Irish (person)	**(der) Ire (m)**
	(die) Irin (f)
Irish (adj. and lang.)	**irisch (-er, -e, -es)**
iron (metal)	**(das) Eisen**
is	**ist**
Israel	**Israel**
Israeli *n.*	**Israeli (m/f)**
Israeli *adj.*	**israelisch (-er, -e, -es)**
it (as subject)	**(der, die, das) – er, sie. es**
it (as object)	**(den, die, das) – ihn, sie, es**
Italian *n.*	**Italiener (m)**
	Italienerin (f)
Italian (adj. and lang.)	**italienisch (-er, -e, -es)**
Italy	**Italien**
January	**(der) Januar**
Japan	**Japan**
Japanese (person)	**(der) Japaner (m)**
	(die) Japanerin (f)
Japanese (adj. and lang.)	**japanisch (-er, -e, -es)**
jewel	**(der) Edelstein**
jewelry	**(der) Schmuck**
job	**(die) Stellung**
joke	**(der) Witz**
July	**(der) Juli**
June	**(der) Juni**
just *adv.*	**soeben**
keep	**behalten**
key	**(der) Schlüssel**
kilometer	**(der) Kilometer**
kind	**freundlich**
(to) know (something)	**wissen**
(to) know (a person)	**kennen**
Korea	**Korea**
Korean *n.*	**Koreaner (m)**
	Koreanerin (f)
lady	**(die) Dame**
(to) land	**landen**
late	**spät**
later	**später**
lawyer	**(der) Rechtsanwalt**

(to) learn	**lernen**
legal	**gesetzlich/legal**
letter	**(der) Brief**
letter of credit	**(der) Kreditbrief**
(irrevocable)	**unwiderruflich (-er, -e, -es)**
license *n.*	**(die) Lizenz**
list	**(die) Liste**
listen	**zuhören**
liter	**(der) Liter**
(a) little	**ein wenig**
loan	**(die) Anleihe/(der) Kredit**
long	**lang (-er, -e, es)**
loss	**(der) Verlust**
loudspeaker	**(der) Lautsprecher**
luck	**(das) Glück**
lunch	**(das) Mittagessen**
machine	**(die) Maschine**
machinery	**(die) Maschinen**
mail	**(die) Post**
(to) mail	**senden**
(to) make	**machen**
manager	**(der) Leiter**
(to) manufacture	**herstellen/fertigen**
manufacturer	**(der) Fabrikant/Hersteller**
many	**viele**
how many?	**wieviele?**
March	**(der) März**
mark (German currency)	**(die) Deutsche Mark/D-Mark**
market	**(der) Markt**
mass production	**(die) Massenproduktion**
material	**(das) Material**
may I ...?	**darf ich ...?**
May	**(der) Mai**
maybe	**vielleicht**
me	**mich**
to me	**mir**
with me	**mit mir**
meat	**(das) Fleisch**
mechanic	**(der) Mechaniker**
(to) meet	**treffen**
meeting	**(die) Versammlung/Sitzung**
menu	**(die) Speisekarte**
merchandise	**(die) Ware**
message	**(die) Botschaft/Nachricht**
meter	**(der) Meter**

milk	(die) Milch
million	(die) Million
minute	(die) Minute
mistake	(der) Fehler
model	(das) Modell
modern	modern (-er, -e, -es)
Monday	(der) Montag
month	(der) Monat
more	mehr
(once) more	noch einmal
morning	(der) Morgen
in the morning	morgens
motor	(der) Motor
motorcycle	(das) Motorrad
movies	(das) Kino
Mr.	Herr
Mrs.	Frau
much	viel
how much?	wieviel?
must (v. aux.)	müssen
I must	ich muß
one must not	man darf nicht
music	(die) Musik
my	mein (m); meine (f); mein (n)
name	(der) Name
last name	(der) Zuname
narrow	eng (-er, -e, -es)
nation	(die) Nation
near	nah/in der Nähe
necessary	wichtig
(to) need	brauchen
I need	ich brauche
we need	wir brauchen
net weight	(das) Nettogewicht
never	nie, niemals
never mind!	macht nichts!
new	neu
news	(die) Nachrichten (pl.)
newspaper	(die) Zeitung
next	nächst (-er, -e, -es)
night	(die) Nacht
nine	neun
nineteen	neunzehn
ninety	neunzig
no	nein

nobody	niemand
noise	(das) Geräusch
noon	(der) Mittag
north	(der) Norden
North America	Nordamerika
Norway	Norwegen
Norwegian *n.*	(der) Norweger (m)
	(die) Norwegerin (f)
not	nicht
not yet	noch nicht
notary	(der) Notar
(to) note	notieren
nothing	nichts
notify	benachrichtigen
not yet	noch nicht
November	(der) November
now	jetzt
until now	bis jetzt
number	(die) Nummer
occupied	besetzt
ocean	(der) Ozean
October	(der) Oktober
(to) offer	anbieten
office	(das) Büro
official	offiziell (-er, -e, -es)
often	oft
oil	(das) Öl
O.K.	in Ordnung
once	einmal
once more	noch einmal
open	offen
(to) open	öffnen
opinion	(die) Meinung
opportunity	(die) Gelegenheit
opposite	gegenüber
or	oder
orange juice	(der) Orangensaft
order (commercial)	(die) Bestellung/Order
(to) order	bestellen / ordern
in order to	um zu (followed by verb)
original	original (-er, -e, -es)
other	andere (-er, -e, -es)
(I) ought to	(ich) sollte ...
(plus infinitive)	
(you) ought to	(Sie) sollten ...
(plus infinitive)	

our	**unser**
outside	**außerhalb**
over (above)	**über**
over (finished)	**vorbei**
(to) owe	**schulden**
(to) own	**besitzen**
owner	**(der) Besitzer**
(to) pack	**einpacken**
package	**(das) Paket/Päckchen**
paid	**bezahlt**
paid in advance	**im voraus bezahl**t
pain	**(der) Schmerz**
paint	**(die) Farbe**
palace	**(der) Palast**
paper	**(das) Papier**
(to) park	**parken**
part	**(der) Teil**
partner	**(der) Teilhaber**
passenger	**(der) Passagier**
passport	**(der) Paß**
(to) pay	**zahlen**
payment	**(die) Zahlung**
peace	**(der) Friede**
pen	**(der) Kugelschreiber**
penalty	**(die) Bestrafung**
pencil	**(der) Bleistift**
people	**(die) Leute**
percent	**(das) Prozent**
perfect	**perfekt -er, -e, -es**
perfume	**(das) Parfüm**
perhaps	**vielleicht**
permit	**(die) Erlaubnis**
permitted	**erlaubt**
person	**(die) Person**
photograph	**(das) Foto**
picture	**(das) Bild**
pill	**(die) Tablette**
plan	**(der) Plan**
plane (airplane)	**(das) Flugzeug**
plant (factory)	**(die) Fabrik**
(to) play	**spielen**
pleasant	**angenehm (-er, -e, -es)**
please!	**bitte!**
Poland	**Polen**
Pole *n.*	**(der) Pole (m)**

	(die) Polin (f)
police	(die) Polizei
policeman	(der) Polizist
Polish (adj. and lang.)	polnisch (-er, -e, -es)
polite	höflich
politics	(die) Politik
poor	arm
port	(der) Hafen
possible	möglich (-er, -e, -es)
postcard	(die) Postkarte
post office	(das) Postamt
potato	(die) Kartoffel
(to) prefer	bevorzugen
prepaid	vorausbezahlt
(to) prepare	vorbereiten
president	(der) Präsident
	(die) Präsidentin
price	(der) Preis
private	privat (-er, -e, -es)
probably	wahrscheinlich
problem	(das) Problem
production	(die) produktion
profession	(der) Beruf
profit	(der) Gewinn
program	(das) Programm
(to) promise	versprechen
promotion	(die) Beförderung
property	(der) Besitz
public	öffentlich (-er, -e, -es)
publisher	(der) Verleger/Verlag
(to) pull	ziehen
purchase order	die Bestellung
(to) push	schieben/drücken
(to) put (into)	setzen/stellen
quality	(die) Qualität
quantity	(die) Menge
question	(die) Frage
quick	schnell
quiet	ruhig (-er, -e, -es)
quite	ganz/ziemlich
race (contest)	(das) Rennen
radio	(das) Radio
railroad	(die) Eisenbahn
raincoat	(der) Regenmantel

rarely	**selten**
rate (of exchange)	**(der) Wechselkurs**
(to) read	**lesen**
ready (finished)	**fertig (-er, -e, -es)**
real	**wirklich**
receipt	**(die) Quittung**
(to) receive	**bekommen/erhalten**
recently	**kürzlich**
(to) recognize	**erkennen**
(to) recommend	**empfehlen**
red	**rot (-er, -e, -es)**
refrigerator	**(der) Kühlschrank**
(to) refuse	**ablehnen**
(my) regards to ...	**beste Grüße an ...**
(to) remain	**bleiben**
(to) remember	**sich erinnern**
(to) rent	**mieten**
(to) repair	**reparieren**
(to) repeat	**wiederholen**
representative	**(der) Vertreter**
research	**(die) Forschung**
reservation	**(die) Reservierung**
restaurant	**(das) Restaurant**
(to) return	**zurückkommen**
rich	**reich (-er, -e, -es)**
(to) ride (in a vehicle)	**fahren**
right (correct)	**richtig (-er, -e, -es)**
(to the) right	**rechts**
right away	**sofort**
ring (jewelry)	**(der) Ring**
river	**(der) Fluß**
road	**(die) Straße**
room (in house)	**(das) Zimmer**
room (space)	**(der) Platz**
round trip	**(die) Rundreise**
route	**(die) Strecke**
rum	**(der) Rum**
(to) run	**laufen**
Russia	**Rußland**
Russian *n.*	**(der) Russe (m)/(die) Russin (f)**
Russian (adj. and lang.)	**russisch (-er, -e, -es)**
safe (locked box)	**(der) Safe**
safe (adj.)	**sicher (-er, -e, -es)**
salary	**(das) Gehalt**
salt	**(das) Salz**

(the) same	derselbe, dieselbe, dasselbe
sample	(das) Muster
satisfied	zufrieden (-er, -e, -es)
Saturday	Samstag (m)
sausage	(die) Wurst
(to) say	sagen
school	(die) Schule
science	(die) Wissenschaft
Scotland	Schottland
Scot n.	(der) Schotte (m)/(die) Schottin (f)
Scottish adj.	schottisch
seat	(der) Sitz
secretary	(der) Sekretär (m)/(die) Sekretärin (f)
(to) see	sehen
seldom	selten
(to) sell	verkaufen
(to) send	senden/schicken
(to) separate	trennen
September	(der) September
(to) settle a bill	eine Rechnung begleichen
seven	sieben
seventeen	siebzehn
seventy	siebzig
several	mehrere
shape	(die) Form
share (stock)	(die) Aktie
she	sie
ship	(das) Schiff
(to) ship (merchandise)	senden
shipment	(die) Sendung
shop	(das) Geschäft
short	kurz (-er, -e, -es)
(I, he, she) should	ich, er, sie sollte
(you, we, they) should	Sie, wir, sie sollten
(to) show	zeigen
show me ...	zeigen Sie mir ...
(to) shut	schließen
silver	(das) Silber
simple	einfach (-er, -e, -es)
please sit down!	nehmen Sie doch Platz!
six	sechs
sixteen	sechzehn
sixty	sechzig
size	(die) Größe
slowly	langsam
small	klein (-er, -e, -es)

so	**so**
soap	**(die) Seife**
some (a little)	**ein bißchen**
somebody	**jemand**
something	**etwas**
sometimes	**manchmal**
somewhere	**irgendwo**
son	**(der) Sohn**
soon	**bald**
(I am) sorry	**es tut (mir) leid**
south	**(der) Süden**
South America	**Südamerika**
South American (*adj.*)	**südamerikanisch (-er, -e, -es)**
Spain	**Spanien**
Spaniard	**Spanier (m)**
	Spanierin (f)
Spanish (adj. and lang.)	**spanisch (-er, -e, -es)**
(to) speak	**sprechen**
special	**besonder (-er, -e, -es)**
(to) spend	**ausgeben**
sport	**(der) Sport**
spring (season)	**(der) Frühling**
stamp (postage)	**(die) Briefmarke**
(to) start	**anfangen**
station (train)	**(der) Bahnhof**
(to) stay	**bleiben**
steel	**(der) Stahl**
stock market	**(die) Börse**
(to) stop	**halten**
the stop (bus, etc.)	**(die) Haltestelle**
store/shop	**(das) Geschäft**
straight ahead	**geradeaus**
street	**(die) Straße**
(to) study	**studieren**
style	**(der) Stil**
subway	**(die) Untergrundbahn/U-Bahn**
success	**(der) Erfolg**
successor	**(der) Nachfolger**
speech	**(die) Rede**
sugar	**(der) Zucker**
summer	**(der) Sommer**
Sunday	**(der) Sonntag**
Sweden	**Schweden**
Swedish (lang. and adj.)	**schwedish (-er, -e, -es)**
Swiss (person)	**(der) Schweizer (m)**
	(die) Schweizerin (f)

Switzerland	(die) Schweiz
Swiss (*adj.*)	schweizerisch (-er, -e, -es)
system	(das) System
table	(der) Tisch
(to) take	nehmen
(to) talk	reden
tank	(der) Tank
tape (adhesive)	(der) Tesafilm/(das) Klebeband
tape recorder	(das) Aufnahmegerät
tariff	(der) Tarif
tax	(die) Steuer
technical	technisch (-er, -e, -es)
(to) telephone	telefonieren
telephone	(das) Telefon
telephone operator	(die) Telefonistin/Vermittlung
television	(das) Fernsehen
temporary	vorübergehend (-er, -e, -es)
ten	zehn
terms	(die) Bedingungen
territory	(das) Gebiet
textile	(das) Gewebe
thank you	danke schön
the	der, die, das
then	dann
there	da
(to) think	denken
thirteen	dreizehn
thirty	dreißig
(what is) this?	(was ist) das?
thousand	tausend
three	drei
Thursday	(der) Donnerstag
ticket (for trains)	(die) Fahrkarte
tip (money)	(das) Trinkgeld
today	heute
together	zusammen
toilet	(die) Toilette
tomorrow	morgen
topic	(das) Thema
total	gesamt (-er, -e, -es)
town	(die) Stadt
traffic	(der) Verkehr
train	(der) Zug
(to) transfer	übertragen
(to) translate	übersetzen

translation	(die) Übersetzung
travel agency	(das) Reisebüro
truck	(der) Lastwagen
Tuesday	(der) Dienstag
Turk *n.*	(ein) Türke (m)
	(eine) Türkin (f)
Turkey	(die) Türkei
Turkish *adj.*	türkisch (-er, -e, -es)
twelve	zwölf
twenty	zwanzig
two	zwei
typist	(die) Schreibmaschinenkraft
umbrella	(der) Regenschirm
uncomfortable	unbequem (-er, -e, -es)
(to) understand	verstehen
do you understand?	verstehen Sie?
unfortunately	unglücklicherweise/leider
union	(die) Vereinigung
trade union	(die) Gewerkschaft
unit	(die) Einheit
United Nations	(die) Vereinten Nationen
United States	(die) Vereinigten Staaten
until	bis
unusual	ungewöhnlich (-er, -e, -es)
up	hinauf
up to now	bis jetzt
urgent	dringend (-er, -e, -es)
(to) use	gebrauchen
useful	nützlich (-er, -e, -es)
usually	üblicherweise
vacant	frei (-er, -e, -es)
valuable	wertvoll (-er, -e, -es)
value	(der) Wert
variety	(die) Abwechselung
very	sehr
very much	sehr viel
very well	sehr gut
vice-president	(der) Vizepräsident
vicinity	(die) Nachbarschaft
visa	(das) Visum
visit	(der) Besuch
(to) visit	besuchen
voyage	(die) Reise
(to) wait	warten

waiter	**(der) Kellner**
waitress	**(die) Kellnerin**
(to) walk	**laufen**
wallet	**(die) Brieftasche**
(to) want to ...	**wollen/möchten (more polite)**
I want to ...	**ich will/möchte**
he (she) wants to	**er (sie) will/möchte**
What do you want?	**Was wünchen Sie?**
war	**(der) Krieg**
warehouse	**(das) Lager**
was	**war**
I (he, she, it) was	**ich (er, sie, es) war**
watch (timepiece)	**(die) Uhr**
(to) watch	**zusehen**
watch out!	**paß auf!**
water	**(das) Wasser**
way	**(der) Weg**
we	**wir**
weak	**schwach**
(to) wear	**tragen**
weather	**(das) Wetter**
Wednesday	**(der) Mittwoch**
week	**(die) Woche**
weight	**(das) Gewicht**
welcome	**willkommen**
you are welcome!	**Sie sind willkommen!**
you (we, they) were	**Sie (wir, sie) waren**
west	**(der) Westen**
what	**was**
what's the matter?	**was ist los?**
what time is it?	**wie spät ist es?**
at what time?	**um wieviel Uhr?**
when?	**wann?**
where?	**wo?**
which?	**welch (-er, -e, -es)**
while	**während**
white	**weiß**
who?	**wer?**
who	**der, die, das**
whose?	**wessen?**
why?	**warum?**
wide	**breit**
wife	**(die) Ehefrau**
will (future of "to be")	**werden (followed by infinitive of verb)**
(to) win	**gewinnen**
winter	**(der) Winter**

wish	(der) Wunsch
(to) wish	wünschen
with	mit
without	ohne
wolf	(der) Wolf
woman	(die) Frau
word	(das) Wort
work	(die) Arbeit
(to) work	arbeiten
world	(die) Welt
(don't) worry!	(keine) Angst!
would you like ...?	Möchten Sie ...?
I would like ...	Ich möchte gern ...
(to) write	schreiben
write it down, please	könnten Sie das bitte aufschreiben?
wrong	falsch (-er, -e, -es)
X-ray	(das) Röntgen
year	(das) Jahr
yellow	gelb
yes	ja
yesterday	gestern
you (sing.)	du (familiar form of address)
you (plur.)	ihr (familiar form of address)
you (sing. and plur.)	Sie (polite form of address)
young	jung
your	dein, deine, dein (familiar form when addressing one person)
	euer, eure, euer (familiar form when addressing more than one person)
	Ihr, Ihre, Ihr (polite form)
zero	(die) Null
zipper	(der) Reißverschluß
zone	(die) Zone
zoo	(der) Zoo